AMERICAN CIVILIZATION

AMERICAN CIVILIZATION

CHARLES A. JONES

INSTITUTE FOR THE STUDY OF THE
AMERICAS
UNIVERSITY OF LONDON · SCHOOL OF ADVANCED STUDY

British Library Cataloguing–in–Publication Data
A catalogue record for this book is available
from the British Library

ISBN   978 1 900039 82 6

INSTITUTE FOR THE STUDY OF THE
AMERICAS
UNIVERSITY OF LONDON · SCHOOL OF ADVANCED STUDY

Institute for the Study of the Americas
31 Tavistock Square
London
WC1H 9HA
Telephone: 020 7862 8870
Fax: 020 7862 8886
Email: americas@sas.ac.uk
Web: www.americas.sas.ac.uk

Buenos Aires was constantly reminding me of Brooklyn.[1]

[1]   Katherine S. Dreier, *Five Months in the Argentine from a Woman's Point of View: 1918 to 1919* (New York, 1920), p. 265, quoted by Beatriz Sarlo in 'The Modern City: Buenos Aires, the Peripheral Metropolis,' in Vivian Schelling, (ed.), *Through the Kaleidoscope: the Experience of Modernity in Latin America* (London and New York, 2000), p. 109.

To Robert Skidelsky
Colleague, Friend and Teacher

CONTENTS

Acknowledgements

This essay grew out of a much shorter paper written for the first World International Studies Conference at Istanbul in the summer of 2005 and read to seminars in Cambridge and at the Institute for the Study of the Americas, London University, in October of that year. It was James Dunkerley, at the ISA, who encouraged me to develop the argument, and he has been a source of great encouragement. I am also grateful to a number of colleagues for their comments on the original paper or parts of this longer version and for helping with useful references. These include Duncan Bell, Ann Keith, Jeremy Wong, Philip Towle, Benjamin de Carvalho, Suzie Hoelgaard and Shogo Suzuki as well as Loraine Macmillan and other members of the Ph.D. colloquium in the Centre of International Studies, Cambridge. My wife Linda put up with several lost weekends toward the end and helped sustain me. I must also thank Mike Sewell and Matthew Brown, both of whom I let down along the way, for their forbearance.

Charles Jones, February 2007, Cambridge.

CHAPTER I

An Obvious Distinction?
The USA and Latin America

Challenging Exceptionality

There are several ways in which the United States of America and the mainland republics to the south of it resemble one another much more than the European monarchies that founded them so long ago. These shared characteristics span the whole range of politics, including the development of nation, state, economy, law and force as well as of attitudes toward each of these, to collective identity, and to history in general. Together they suggest that the United States may best be regarded as more American than Western or European, let alone British, just as Brazil is far more than Portugal writ large and neither Mexico nor Argentina can be adequately understood as outgrowths of Spain.

To outline a hemispheric American culture and appreciate its peculiar character might be thought a worthy objective in its own right. It may also help account for the distinctive approach to international relations that has developed in the Americas since independence. This in turn may make it easier to follow ways in which this approach has changed over time, to specify more clearly some of the hemispheric norms from which the United States has deviated since it became a world power, and to describe the trajectories of a US drift toward imperialism, neo-mercantilism and militarism which now has global implications.

More parochially, to make it clear that the United States makes policy as an American, rather than an English-speaking or quasi-European power, promises to disabuse the British of their nostalgic fixation with a special relationship which, from the other side of the Atlantic, must seem just one of a number of casual affairs, resumed with bemused affection from time to time when the old lady takes the trouble to doll herself up.

There is not the least intention here to deny what is obviously true. Unipolarity, the continuing and intensive intercourse between Europe and the

Americas, and the relatively greater success of political liberalism in the United States and Canada than in the rest of the hemisphere are all taken for granted.

The United States today is unique in many ways. Though no longer industrially dominant to anything like the extent that it was in the mid-twentieth century, it remains far wealthier than any other country in the Western hemisphere, even Canada, which is in any case largely dependent upon its neighbour. Militarily, it is currently supreme and has been maintaining levels of expenditure sufficient to sustain its superiority for another generation, barring disaster. Its corporations and their brands are still salient in world markets. Its currency, no longer pivotal, is nevertheless accepted in daily transactions in many other states, acts as a reserve currency, and is the medium of exchange for many trans-border exchanges between third parties, including worldwide transactions in petroleum. Its popular culture exerts huge influence on aspirations and behaviour across more than half the globe, perhaps even more for the rising generation than for their parents. Its political and economic systems and the values that underpin them are among the most attractive in the world, as is evident from the press of humanity at its frontiers. In all these respects the USA is without doubt exceptional, whether compared to other American states, to erstwhile 'world empires' such as Rome or China, or to states that were great powers not so long ago or might now be thought aspirants to that status, such as France, Russia and Britain on the one hand, or China, Japan, Brazil and India on the other.

None of this is at issue. Rather, the question is whether the United States is *sui generis* – a power utterly without parallel not only quantitatively but also qualitatively – or else remains attached by common culture and shared experience to some larger grouping of states, and – if so – which.

Shortly after the end of the Cold War, Samuel P. Huntington argued that the USA might continue to lead a West redefined in cultural rather than ideological terms. [2] (By the West is generally meant Western Europe and the temperate-zone states of predominantly European settlement.) It is undeniable that the United States and its American neighbours still enjoy close and often fruitful relations with their founding nations. They bear substantial traces of European customs and cultures. Indeed, it is in some respects they, and not the lands of their parents, that have conserved traditions eroded by modernization in Europe. Think only of the survival of British folk music in the Alleghenies and of Cajun music in Louisiana or the relative purity of Spanish as spoken in parts of Andean South America when compared, say, with Andalucia. Just as often the cultural tide has swept back across the Atlantic, bearing tobacco, chocolate, tomatoes, turkey, samba, potatoes, tango, cocktails, rap, CNN and the blues.

---

[2]   Samuel P. Huntington, *The Clash of Civilizations and the Remaking of World Order* (New York, 1997).

All this traffic makes it easy for Europeans to feel themselves at home in the Americas and for Americans to feel at home in Iberia or Britain. Language helps, both directly and through the exchange of television, novels, and films. Yet it is seldom very long before a chance remark or encounter reveals some chasm of cultural difference. It may be happening upon a trailer park, which immediately spells poverty and migrant labour to Europeans but has a more complex and ambiguous social meaning in the United States. It may be a first encounter with rural Louisiana or one of the rougher and more abandoned neighbourhoods of inner-city Chicago or Philadelphia, closer to the stereotypical European image of Latin America than of the USA.[3] Or take the prosperous middle-aged farmer from the midwest of the United States who travelled by rail across the seventy or eighty miles of English countryside that separate the conurbations of London and the West Midlands, gazing at the landscape with rapt attention, before turning to his wife to utter the single word – 'Cauliflowers!' Why, he continued, had not all this eminently suitable little patch of land been turned over to their production on a grand scale?

To repeat, there is no denying the importance of such links as remain between Europe and America. It is simply that the USA may better be regarded as one among many American states, sharing more – and more important – characteristics with its neighbours to the South than with other nations.

Finally, it can hardly be denied that the British colonies in North America already possessed, in their pre-independence constitutions and economies, germs of representative government and complex inter-regional trade that would prove more robust in the aftermath of political revolution than the administrative divisions and complex fiscal interdependence of the Spanish Empire. So the claim advanced here is certainly not that American states are identical, but rather that they bear a family resemblance to one another and have been engaged in a shared project: trying to accomplish a similar set of tasks in varying yet comparable circumstances, with greater or lesser resources, some competently, others less so. In briefest terms that project has consisted in the development of a liberal political and economic order within highly racialized societies. It is, as yet, by no means complete.

---

[3] Toward the end of the twentieth century 10 per cent of all dwellings in the USA, housing 12.5 million people, were mobile homes. In 1985 mobile homes accounted for 20 per cent of all new houses sold in the USA. Stewart Brand, *How Buildings Learn: What Happens After They're Built* (London & New York, 1995), p. 153. It must be noted that trailers do not necessarily spell poverty. At the time of writing (September 2006) and at the upper end of the market, trailers can be very costly in hot spots: over $1 million in Malibu and topping $500,000 in Key West, not including land, for which a hefty monthly rent is paid. Yet we're still talking about trailers, and about people who can afford no better in the locations where they want or need to live.

The Power of Language

One of the ways in which power works most effectively is through language. Once a visionary has people talking as though utopia were a real possibility the battle is half won. Conversely, one of the most insidious forms in which power can be exerted is by making it hard to say or think things that challenge the natural or commonsense view. To claim that the United States of America is a deviant Latin American country would rightly be regarded as inaccurate and doubly offensive as well as counter-intuitive. It would be inaccurate because, with due respect for a tiny Cajun minority and a rather larger minority of recent Hispanic migrants from Latin America, the USA is not predominantly Latin in culture. It would be offensive to Latin Americans and US citizens alike because each of the many American republics has its own distinctive political identity, often defined partly by contrast or rivalry with one or more of the others. It would be counterintuitive because it will seem obvious to most readers that the USA, if not entirely *sui generis*, should be judged against other mature and industrialized liberal democracies, and not the twenty or so republics to the south of it. Yet something very much like this is exactly what needs to be said, and the ways in which language and entrenched habits of thought impede this is as good a place as any to begin the story.

In the first place, the easy appropriation of 'America' as the common name for the USA in English is so routine that to try to avoid it is almost impossible, most of all for lack of a neat alternative to 'Americans' when referring to its inhabitants or citizens. But the ease with which the mind identifies America and the United States of American is such that to claim that the USA is a deviant *American* state just won't cut the mustard. Most readers would read and re-read and still be uncertain, mainly because an American state is (isn't it?) a state of the Union. The pre-eminence of the USA within the English-speaking world has effectively deprived the language of an adjective that gathers together all the countries in the Western hemisphere. Rolling over carelessly in her sleep, the sow has smothered the lustiest of the piglets, and we are left with South American, Central American, North American, Caribbean, Hispanic-American, Luso-American, Francophone, Anglophone, hemispheric and Latin American, to mention just a few of a not inconsiderable litter of adjectives, and we get along all right most of the time, though not when the task is to suggest that there is a shared American history and a common American political culture, or that the United States is or is not typically American.

Even after it has been made clear that what is standing on the tarmac is a suggestion that the Americas be treated as a single unit of historical and political analysis, many readers will still be reluctant to climb on board, since division between Latin and Anglo-America has come to seem so natural to them. Why should anyone abandon the commonsense view? The answer is that what appears obvious and uncontroversial here, as so often happens, is the product of prolonged political and social struggle. It may be possible to reveal how tangled and problematic this particular bit of common sense is by posing two questions. How did it come to seem so natural to divide the hemisphere into two worlds, Latin and Anglo-Saxon? Why are the foundations of this division no longer secure? The task of the first part of this essay is therefore to lay bare the extent to which the seemingly natural division came about as a consequence of the play of Great Power politics, to explain how, once established, it was bound to relegate any twentieth-century project of a common American history to the sidelines, and to sketch some ways in which recent historiographic revisions have eaten away at its foundations.

Back on Track: Too Late

It is ironic that the naturalization of the Latin-Anglo distinction should have come about precisely when it did, the process being more or less complete by 1890. For it can certainly be argued that it was between about 1860 and 1890 that Spanish America and Brazil finally emerged from a period of relative economic stagnation to resume sustained rates of economic growth approximating those of the Anglophone north. As it did so, the South attracted a veritable flood of investment from Europe, up to 1914, of just the sort that had been pouring into the USA shortly before.[4] This was also the point at which the fragmentation, factionalism and *caudillismo* that had marked political life in the first two generations after independence gave way to constitutional regimes ordered on liberal principles in many of the republics and when, at last, monarchy gave way finally and irrevocably to republic in Mexico and Brazil.

Such transformations as these might have been expected to lead, by the close of the nineteenth century, to the Americas being thought of as constituting a relatively homogeneous and distinctive realm, very much as most of those who fought for independence throughout the hemisphere in the half-century

---

[4]   John H. Coatsworth, 'Economic and Institutional Trajectories in Nineteenth-Century Latin America,' in John H. Coatsworth and Alan M. Taylor (eds.), *Latin America and the World Economy since 1800* (Cambridge MA, 1998). For all its merits, Coatsworth's study pays little attention to the relative economic effects of warfare in North and South America. Nor is it as clear as one might wish, because of the small size and composition of his sample (p. 26, Table 1.1), to what extent the damage was done before or after 1800. This point is discussed later.

beginning 1776 would have wished and expected. So, indeed, the rise of the Inter-American system of international relations and the attempt to develop a body of *American* law as the vanguard of positive international law would suggest.[5] Witness also the alacrity with which British capitalists of a liberal disposition moved southward to the River Plate republics after the Civil War in search of an extra half-a-per-cent, confidently envisaging them as a new USA.

To the Morrisons, Radical plutocrats in the van of this migration of capital, the hemisphere appeared but a single republican project. Investment was not just about money; it was about the building of a new world. Such was the republican commitment of Walter Morrison, Chairman of the Central Argentine Railway Company, that he banned French wines and spirits from his cellars during the Second French Empire (1852–1870), substituting Chianti from newly united Italy and Jerusalem brandy, while the family lawyer – William Ashurst – hosted Guiseppe Mazzini to lunch fortnightly during his exile in London. His partner, John Morris, contrasted the commitment of his group's 'application of capital to the development of the natural resources of the country' with what he termed 'the abuse of capital [by] those that deal in government loans, concessions etc. [and] go to make pots of money'.[6]

Two Civilizations or One?

In a world parallel to and not very different from our own, it would have seemed obvious to some hypothetical Samuel Huntington by the 1990s, after a century of sustained growth at similar rates in North and South America, that there was a single *American* civilization, equally distinct from Sinic, Orthodox, Islamic, *and* West European civilizations, rather than a Western civilization in which the USA was conjoined with Western Europe, Australia and (some) other lands of European settlement, yet divided from the American states to its South: a West, indeed, of which Catholic Iberians until recently under prolonged authoritarian rule were a part, while their American cousins were excluded for lesser lapses from democracy.

If Protestantism of the kind supposedly embedded in institutions and practices of the British colonies was to account for the distinctiveness and success of the

---

[5] Francis A. Boyle, *Foundations of World Order: the legalist approach to international relations, 1898–1922* (Durham, NC, and London, 1999). Boyle is quite clear about the racism of US international lawyers and statesmen of the late-nineteenth century but equally clear, in chapter 6 (p. 104 ff), about US commitment to 'the formation of an inter-American system . . . that was intended to be distinct from and superior to the European balance-of-power system'.

[6] Charles A. Jones, *International Business in the Nineteenth Century: the Rise and Fall of a Cosmopolitan Bourgeoisie* (Brighton, 1987), p. 91.

United States, why were the negative implications of Catholicism for Latin America not a more continuous and consistent influence? More broadly, if the distinction between Protestant and Catholic is less stark than used to be thought, why should Latin America be regarded, as it was in Huntington's famous 'Clash of Civilizations' article and the subsequent book, as a distinct civilization, alongside Western, Islamic, Sinic, Japanese, Hindu, Orthodox, Buddhist and African.[7] Why, in any case, was Huntington happy to include Catholic Italy, Spain and Portugal in the West, none of them exemplary democracies, but not Latin America? The answer is that Huntington felt that Catholicism, Corporatism and persistent indigenous cultures together set Latin America aside from the West as at the very least a sub-culture.

This may be the moment to identify four features of Huntington's arguments that depend on historical narratives that are to be challenged in the remainder of this chapter. 'Europe and North America both felt the effects of the Reformation' – Huntington assures his readers – 'and have combined Catholic and Protestant cultures.' Correct to a point; but while it will be argued here that the distinction between Catholicism and Protestantism as sources of economic and political development has been exaggerated, it is nevertheless true that subjective religious convictions were such that Europe would achieve this 'combination' only after centuries of ostensibly religious warfare and persecution, and then only partially. Beyond the cities, much of Southern Europe has remained staunchly Catholic. Even in liberal Britain Catholic emancipation in 1829 preceded the abolition of slavery in British colonies by only five years and the dedication of a Roman Catholic church in sleepy Cambridge provoked vituperative opposition as recently as 1890.[8] In Europe the 'combination' of which Huntington writes has perhaps been more emulsion than solution, making religiosity a feature that unites the Americas and divides them from Western Europe.

Second, Huntington points out that 'Latin America incorporates indigenous cultures which . . . were effectively wiped out in North America.' This careless swipe of the paw may be taken as a slur on the aboriginal populations of the USA and Canada, of whom in the region of three million still identify themselves as belonging to First Nations or as Native Americans, and who have been organizing with increasing effectiveness over the past half-century, especially in Canada. But even accepting, as one must, the massive death toll imposed by European and creole settlers, the distinction is less between Anglophone North America

---

[7] Huntington, *Clash of Civilizations*, Map 1.3, pp. 26–7.

[8] Philip S. Wilkins, 'Founding a Cambridge Cathedral: Yolande Lyne-Stephens, Canon Christopher Scott and the Church of Our Lady and the English Martyrs,' in Nicholas Rogers (ed.), *Catholics in Cambridge* (Leominster, 2003), pp.100–101. Slavery continued in an India not yet directly subject to the Crown.

and Latin America than between areas of settled and nomadic pre-conquest civilization.[9] The Argentine army were no slouches when it came to genocide. 'Decimation', meaning to put one in ten to death, is often misused. One reaches for a word that really does mean to leave one in ten alive in order to describe the 'desert' campaigns of 1879–84, and even then it would hardly suffice. Close to half a million died, according to some estimates, and the result was a country that had more in common with the United States than any other in the Americas by 1914 in population, production, urbanization and lifestyle, lacking only a significant African-American minority, heavy industry and economies of scale.

Third, the contrast between Latin corporatism and Anglo individualism stands or falls with the stark traditional distinctions between Catholicism and Protestantism, the Weber thesis, and the standard critique of Spanish absolutism. But it must also depend upon contemporary observation. The United States doesn't look so very individualist. Felipe Fernandez-Arnesto puts it with characteristic force and a cynical contempt for what others, myself included, may regard as one of the most attractive features of society in the USA:

> People in the United States are cloyingly gregarious, profoundly
> communitarian, boringly conformist. They get glutinously
> embedded in any community they can, outside their own families:
> the workplace, high school and college alumni associations, the
> neighbourhood, the city, the church . . . Membership is treated as a
> religious obligation; it does not matter what you belong to as long as
> you belong to something . . . Civic-mindedness, not individualism, is
> what makes 'America' great.[10]

Bernard-Henri Lévy concurs, writing of the 'tradition of civic-mindedness and civility – I won't even say of compassion – that was responsible, and continues to be responsible, for this country's greatness.'[11] Nor is it only Europeans who see the United States in this way.[12]

---

[9] Huntington, *Clash of Civilizations*, p. 46. If the terms 'America' and 'Americans' pose problems for a hemispheric history, so too does lack of a single acceptable term to capture those of European descent throughout the continent. This is because 'creole' has, in the United States, a primary reference to white descendants of French settlers in Louisiana and, in England, strong overtones of the Caribbean and of mixed race. I shall use it in spite of this, for want of anything better.

[10] Felipe Fernandez-Arnesto, *The Americas* (2004), p. 161. Could it be that the Atlanta policeman who, by his own account, 'used an excessive amount of discretion' when arresting Fernandez-Arnesto in January 2007 for jay-walking, had read the Professor's work? It's nice to think so.

[11] Bernard-Henri Lévy, *American Vertigo: On the Road from Newport to Guantanamo* (London, 2006).

[12] Robert D. Putnam, *Bowling Alone: the Collapse and Revival of American Community* (New York, 2000).

These criticisms are hardly matters of detail, but perhaps the most interesting feature of Huntington's exclusion of Latin America from the West is his failure to recognize the extent to which the functional similarity between surviving indigenous populations to the South and the African-American minority in his own country link the USA to the rest of the continent and divide it from Western Europe.

Six Pillars of United States Exceptionalism

Cannonades directed at the surface of Huntington's argument have little effect. It can withstand bombardment. It is high time to start mining. Six distinct discourses, each of them rooted in power politics, were to ensure the implausibility of a holistic view of the Americas and guarantee that efforts to cultivate the project of a Continental history in the mid-twentieth century would be largely stillborn. They are French cultivation of a pan-Latin identity, the Black Legend, its development and perpetuation by the Romantics, the Protestant work ethic, scientific racism, and a discourse of United States post-imperialism.

In purely linguistic terms, the difficulty is much like that attending the use, generally by Americans (You see! – The word is indispensable in this sense) of 'England' and 'English' when the intention is to refer to all the countries that comprise the tediously named United Kingdom of Great Britain and Northern Ireland. (How can the British think that anyone has time to bother with a pernickety name like this? One can only suppose that back in 1922 it was still a more leisurely age, at least for the more senior servants of the Crown.) A second example is the use, by Britons and Ulsterfolk, of 'The British Isles'. Even when it is intended as no more than a geographical expression, it is received as a lingering British claim upon the whole of the island of Ireland and is about as welcome as that friendly pat on the bottom from the boss.

Faced with these niceties of expression the common response of English speakers has generally been to dismiss the concerns of the offended groups (Latin Americans, Scots, the Welsh, and citizens of the Republic of Ireland) as mere detail. *Mere* detail!? The devil, we are rightly told, is in the detail. Those who have experienced repression do not need Gramsci to tell them that it is daily acquiescence in such small indignities that provides the ground upon which greater indignities can be heaped. Spanish speakers, having learnt this through bitter experience, coined the rebarbative yet necessary term *'estadounidenses'* (from *estados unidos* – United States) because they are unwilling to exclude themselves from *'americanos'* and there are times when *'gringos'* is just a little too inclusive or a little too much.

Latin Political Identity

So how and why did the English-speaking world get itself into this mess? The French are in part responsible. As well as being the period in which many American states consolidated and began to engage seriously in the formation of integrated economies and the cultivation of national identity, the last third of the nineteenth century turned out, quite coincidentally, to be a point of acute anxiety in French history. French concern at the tightening British grip on sub-Saharan Africa and South and East Asia and the rapidly growing industrial power of the United States, to say nothing of the consolidation of new nation-states on its borders, in Germany and Italy, led to self-conscious attempts to cultivate linguistic commonalities that might serve as the basis for a coalition to balance Anglo-Saxondom.

This is why the word 'Latin' started to be used in a geopolitical sense only in the 1860s. The new usage indeed appears to have originated in France itself, where a 'Pan-Latin' foreign policy was proposed in order to rally countries with predominantly Roman Catholic populations and languages deriving directly from Latin against Russian (Slav) and British (Anglo-Saxon) expansionism.

This *démarche* yielded one or two nuggets, among them the Latin Union or monetary system formed by France, Belgium, Italy and Switzerland in 1865. It had pretty much petered out by the time of the 1884 Spanish proposal that a Latin League be formed to check the growing power of Germany, but not before it had had a curious and unintended linguistic consequence, as more and more people began to distinguish between an Anglo north and a Latin south in the Americas. 'Latin America' appears to have gained currency in English only in the 1880s around the time that the pejorative 'dago' escaped from sailors' argot or South-Western United States regional usage into the general and metropolitan vocabulary.[13] It did so, in short, at a time when the tide of scientific racism was rising, leading to a deterioration in relations between Anglophones and the rest, which the French initiative merely aggravated. Moreover, it was seized upon gleefully – if naively – by francophile *criollo* elites in the recently independent American states as an element in their own political project, since it 'lifted up the population of European descent and erased the Indian and the Afro populations'.[14] In short, a distinction that served local racisms, North and South, ironically had negative consequences for relations between racist elites.

---

[13] J. David Dressing, 'Latin America,' in Barbara A. Tennebaum (ed.), *Encyclopedia of Latin American History and Culture*, vol. III (1996), p. 390. José Martí heard the word used of Sicilians and noted this in 'The Lynching of the Italians,' [March 1891]: *José Martí: Selected Writings* (Harmsworth, 2002), p. 299.
[14] Walter D. Mignolo, *The Idea of Latin America* (Oxford, 2005), p. 59.

The Black Legend

Once the naming has been done, half the work of discrimination is accomplished. With an appropriate vocabulary neatly stacked at intervals along the way, the road is open for the historians, the narrators, to lay a carefully graded ribbon of intellectual tarmac across the countryside, calculated to guide thought in ways most convenient to those who rule. A familiar story unfolds. The United States is exceptional because it was founded by Puritans who brought with them an individualism born out of the direct post-Reformation relationship between individual and God. Protestantism had deprived the priesthood of their role as mediators, controlling holy texts and absolution. Presbyterians were among the more extreme or Puritan groups that wished to dispense with bishops entirely. James I of England, alarmed by their rising fortunes, prophesied: 'No bishop; no king'. His successor, Charles I, was beheaded in 1649, just four years after reluctantly sacrificing his Archbishop of Canterbury, William Laud (1573–1645), to his Puritan and Parliamentary opponents.

Subsequent events would reverse many of the gains of the English Revolution. The monarchy and an Episcopalian church were restored, and rising industrial power led the corrupt, war-mongering Hanoverian state into an interminable series of wars of aggrandisement. Yet the British colonies in North America, mostly founded by religious dissidents, gained in some measure from an autonomy that arose from the relative weakness and inefficiency of the British state, where the historic compromise of the Glorious Revolution of 1688 had left the monarchy with less than absolute power. When the British hand became heavier and imperial impositions became intolerable, after the Seven Years' War, the Colonies broke loose and embarked on a great liberal experiment. Spanish America, meanwhile, stagnated under the absolutist rule of the Hapsburgs and their Bourbon successors. Treated as a private purse by the Crown, the empire was further oppressed by the Counter-Reformation Roman Catholic Church, with its taxes, its colonialist religious orders and the Inquisition, stifling enterprise, free thought and expression. Innovation and energy became the hallmarks of Anglo-American responses to the New World: replication and nostalgia of Hispanic responses.

If one accepts this version of history, or something like it, then to compare the United States and Latin America is risible, because the first was developed from the start on the basis of a political culture, developing organically out of Protestantism, that was individualistic, law-governed and entrepreneurial, while Spanish America laboured under greedy and overbearing monarchs and the intolerant bishops of Rome who, between them, frustrated the emergence of autonomous political institutions and globally competitive industries.

The story continues. By the eighteenth century the dice were cast. Britain and Spain had been at war intermittently for more than a century. Often, the causes were commercial rivalry or European dynastic and balance-of-power considerations. Underlying them, however, was the religious distinction that had already emerged in the sixteenth century as a cause of war when the English Crown broke with Rome. Though the Anglican settlement was moderate in doctrinal terms, Roman Catholics would continue to be regarded with suspicion in Britain until the nineteenth century, as potential agents of Spain or France. If anything, the prominence of more extreme forms of Protestantism among British migrants to North America coupled with the proximity of the Spanish threat in the Caribbean and Florida and the French in Louisiana and Canada led to an even greater fear of popery in the American colonies. These longstanding enmities were supported on both sides by propaganda, that of Protestants and liberal Spaniards against the Roman Catholic Church being summed up in the so-called Black Legend, with its emphasis on the intolerance and violence of the Inquisition and the severity of Spanish rule in the Indies.

Romanticizing the Legend

Following decisive British victories over the French in the Seven Years' War (1756–1763) and Napoleonic Wars (1792–1815) and the consequent fragmentation of the Spanish empire, Anglophone Americans had little to fear from the old enemies. At the same time the British had now to govern a substantial French-speaking Catholic population in Canada while the newly independent thirteen colonies were, by mid-century, experiencing a much-needed influx of labour from Europe, much of it from staunchly Catholic Ireland.

In the United States, as in Britain, the solution was to romanticize and historicize the founding religious myth, casting it in a form that denigrated an Other no longer present (the Spanish) while allowing the present Other (Catholic immigrants) to display loyalty without unduly compromising conscience.

Spanish Romanticism, in its most reactionary form, strove to apply a cultural apparatus not unlike that of the trumped up Napoleonic Empire to reinvest a restored monarchy and a reinvigorated church with a legitimacy that had been disrupted by the French Revolution of 1789 and its aftermath. It was a task that was to become more and more difficult as modernity took hold of the country through industrialization, mass literacy and media, and the railway. In Britain, where there had been no rupture of legitimacy, the political functions of Romanticism were more understated. They included an emphasis on the countryside as the locus of authentic experience in an increasingly urbanised society, stress – especially in Byron – on the world as canvas for what was now a global power and, above all, a comfortable distancing, in the historical novels of Sir Walter Scott, of threats that were, if truth be told, not entirely exhausted.[15] By dealing with invasion through fictionalized accounts of the final Stuart uprising of 1745, now two generations distant, Scott used the first of his novels, *Waverley* (1814), to cool a threat of invasion that had been all too real only a few years before. Sectarian enmities that were to continue to be a source of social violence on the streets of Belfast, Glasgow and Liverpool right up to the end of the twentieth century were sublimated into costume drama, personalized, and lined up against a range of more domestic dichotomies – between madness and sanity, feminine and masculine – which somehow cut them down to size.

The Waverley novels were hugely successful and much imitated throughout Europe and the Americas. In the United States, Scott's leading disciple, James Fennimore Cooper, turned to eighteenth-century warfare, as Scott had done, to exercise and damp down tensions between the state, colonists, and indigenous Americans. These were far from settled at the time he wrote, yet consigning them to the past could make them seem so, at least to readers in New England. New England was also the ground for two other American experiments in Romanticism. Down by Walden Lake there was Henry David Thoreau (1817–1862), facing the wilderness and practising self-sufficiency within easy walking distance of his patron, Ralph Waldo Emerson (1803–1882), all too reminiscent of the child who leaves home for ever and ever only to camp at the end of the garden. Not far away, New England historians and writers including William Prescott (1796–1859) and Washington Irving (1783–1859) gave quite a fillip to the Black Legend, the former through his pioneering *History of the Conquest of Mexico* (1843) and *Conquest of Peru* (1847) and the latter through his orientalization of Andalucia in *The Conquest of Granada* (1829) and *The Alhambra* (1832), adapting it to modern times by linking the supposedly centralized absolutism of Spain with mercantilism and economic decline and, conversely, the liberty of the North with commercial prosperity and economic growth.[16]

By shifting the original doctrinal distinction between Protestant North and Catholic South more toward politics and economy, the New England historians also prepared the ground for two later pillars of United States exceptionalism. The first was the idea of a National Creed, a term coined in 1944 by Gunnar Myrdal

---

[15] An interesting American foil to this aspect of English Romanticism is the placelessness or spatial insecurity of US Romanticism, discussed in Robert E. Abrams, *Landscape and Ideology in American Renaissance Literature: Topographies of Skepticism* (Cambridge, 2004).

[16] D. A. Brading, *The First America: the Spanish Monarchy, Creole Patriots, and the Liberal State, 1492–1866* (Cambridge, 1991), p. 630–1.

and succinctly rendered sixty years later by Samuel P. Huntington as 'Protestantism without God'.[17] The second was a view of economic history that rooted United States success in the Creed and the institutions in which it had been embedded. Part of an audacious microeconomic imperialism of the 1970s which took rational choice, collective action and Coasean approaches deep into the heartlands of politics, international relations and sociology, this new institutionalist approach was most closely associated with Douglass North.[18] In the 1840s and 50s, many liberals in the new republics to the South shared these views, regarding the market as a historical force superior to that of the Spanish Crown.[19] Vicente Fídel López, Argentine writer and statesman, cast the English as allies of liberty against Spanish mercantilism and the Inquisition in a youthful pirate novel of the 1840s, *La novia del hereje* (*Betrothed to a Heretic*), offering the vision of a politically unified and mixed-race South America that was never to be.[20] But the fatal combination of a romanticized Black Legend and rising scientific racism meant that the Yankees would never appreciate the extent of their political kinship with Latin American liberal elites or succeed in capitalizing upon it.

Prussians and Protestants

It had become orthodoxy, by the early twentieth century, that the economic lead of the north dated back almost to the end of the seventeenth century. The British colonies in North America had been steadily pulling away from the stagnant empire to the South of them. The two distinct political cultures were firmly embedded in institutions that would prove extremely robust, carrying within them the social equivalent of a genetic code that would continue to replicate itself even when Protestant English capitalists attempted the transformation of Latin American economies in the later nineteenth century or migration to the United States become predominantly Catholic and, more recently, American.

---

[17]   Samuel P. Huntington, *Who Are We? – America's Great Debate* (London, 2004), p. 69.

[18]   The key works are Douglass C. North, *Growth and Welfare in the American Past: a New Economic History* (Englewood Cliffs, NJ, 1966); Lance E. Davis and Douglass C. North, *Institutional Change and American Economic Growth* (Cambridge, 1971); Douglass C. North, *Rise of the Western World: a New Economic History* (Cambridge, 1973); and Douglass C. North, *Structure and Change in Economic History* (New York, 1981).

[19]   Charles A. Jones, 'British Capital in Argentine History: Structures, Rhetoric and Change,' in Alistair Hennessy and John King (eds.), *The Land that England Lost: Argentina and Britain, a Special Relationship* (London, 1992a).

[20]   Vicente Fidel López, *La novia del hereje o La inquisición de Lima* [Buenos Aires, 1854] (Buenos Aires, 2001).

We have seen that this combination of cultural and institutional arguments owes much to the Black Legend and depends on some very dubious historical writing, much of it well past its sell-by date, and is therefore implicated in the very rivalries that it claims to describe. In recent years German historians attacking the privileged position claimed by Weber and others for Protestantism within the narrative of German history have inadvertently done much to undermine the Black Legend. Attention has been drawn to the structural similarity of Catholic and Protestant states in the early modern period. Setting aside doctrinal questions, Reformation and Counter-Reformation were not so much distinct, sequential and antagonistic movements as concurrent and functionally similar transformations by which conformity in religious belief served to define populations by the creation of so-called 'confessions' (*Konfessionalisierung*). By this is meant communities of belief that served as proto-nations while emerging states strove to develop ways of co-opting the loyalties of these newly constituted collective subjects.[21]

The Protestant Work Ethic

By its suggestion that processes of social discipline, rationalization and disenchantment were at work in Catholic as well as Protestant states, this confessionalist historiographic revision makes it even more difficult than before to accept the linkage, famously suggested by Max Weber, between Protestantism and a work ethic conducive to rapid economic development. This has always been theologically suspect. Within the Catholic Church the priest mediated between sinner and God, hearing confession, imposing penance and granting absolution. Having set aside mediation and forgone the assurance of salvation deriving from the sacraments and the authority of the Church, the Protestant – so the theory runs – stood in need of some functionally equivalent assurance of salvation and found it in the wealth that came from commercial and industrial enterprise. But might not a good Catholic bourgeois in Languedoc or Galicia just as easily sanctify worldly success by an inventive extension of the Catholic doctrine of justification by works? Doctrine hardly seems to settle the matter.

---

[21] Wolfgang Reinhard, 'Reformation, Counter-Reformation, and the Early Modern State: A Reassessment,' *The Catholic Historical Review*, vol. 75, no. 3 (July 1989), pp. 383–404; Heinz Schilling, 'Confessional Europe,' in Thomas A. Brady, Jr., Heiko A. Oberman and James D. Tracy (eds.), *Handbook of European History, 1400–1600: Late Middle Ages, Renaissance and Reformation*, vol. II: *Visions, Programs and Outcomes* (Leiden, 1995); R. Po-Chia Hsia, *Social Discipline in the Reformation: Central Europe, 1550–1750* (London and New York, 1989).

Most of all, Weber's theory is weak empirically. It is not just that since his day numerous non-Protestant countries such as Japan, the Republic of Ireland or post-Franco Spain have achieved rapid economic growth. It is not just that we now know, as Weber could not, that industry and wealth in England in the eighteenth and nineteenth centuries were much more tied up with the state and the predominantly Anglican (Episcopalian) South East than with private enterprise in the non-conformist northern towns.[22] It is also that Weber could and should have known that the variation his cultural theory claimed to explain could equally well be attributed to the fortunes of war and revolution. By the 1780s the Catalan textile industry was every bit as advanced as anything in Britain. Perhaps it was because of this that the French laid waste to it in 1794.[23] Protestant Britain did well out of the war, and this helped its commerce and industry. The formation and subsequent enlargement of the German Zollverein aided the development of Protestant and Catholic enterprise alike in the German confederation. It was largely the work of Protestant Prussia and was resisted by Catholic Austria, a resistance which culminated in the Austro-Prussian War of 1866 and has left Austria, to this day, a separate, predominantly Catholic, German-speaking country.

Yet religion here was in many ways incidental. It was an Austrian preference for high tariffs that kept it out of the Zollverein, and this cannot be directly pinned on Catholicism. Market size in the British and French Empires, the USA and the Zollverein may have been more important in fostering growth than religious preferences. Nor does religious difference account for the incidence of social revolution in Europe, though it happens that Protestant Britain gained relatively by its narrow avoidance of disruption. It is just too much of a stretch for Weber, or those in the USA who like to rely on him, to argue that Protestantism fosters industry indirectly by first delivering success on the battlefield, diplomatic skill, or social stability, and unless that step is taken Protestant industrial supremacy in the nineteenth century looks pretty contingent.

The Myth of Absolutism

What should prove to be the final nail in the coffin of the Black Legend has been driven in only recently by Regina Grafe and Alejandra Irigoin.[24] They charge

---

[22] W. D. Rubinstein, *Men of Property: the Very Wealthy in Britain since the Industrial Revolution* (London, 1981).

[23] Richard Herr, *Eighteenth-Century Revolution in Spain* (Princeton NJ, 1958), pp. 141 and 381.

[24] Maria Alejandra Irigoin and Regina Grafe, 'Bargaining for Absolutism: A Spanish Path to Nation State and Empire,' *University of Oxford Discussion Papers in Economic and Social History*, no. 65 (2006)

Douglass North and the New Institutional Economics school with having been too trusting of historians of an earlier generation. North readily accepted that Castile and, later, the Spanish empire in the Americas, was a centralized state dependent on the extraction of revenues from the periphery by an extensive and consistent bureaucracy. He contrasted this with a much weaker English state that perforce allowed its American colonies considerable autonomy. Grafe and Irigoin cite a wealth of recent historiography that goes far to soften this contrast and can be summed up in the judgment of that doyen of Argentine historians, Tulio Halperín Donghi, that 'absolutism was an aspiration rather than an effective regime'.[25]

More telling than an accumulation of quantitative judgments in the secondary literature is the detailed empirical research carried out by Grafe and Irigoin on the fiscal system of the Spanish empire toward the end of the eighteenth century. From this flow two important conclusions. The first is that Latin American incomes were considerably higher relative to those in Anglophone America than was once thought, suggesting that divergence took place from about 1800, not 1700. Comparing revenue of $46.3 million collected in the USA during the quinquennium 1796–1800 with the 338 million pesos collected during the same period in New Spain, they conclude that 'even if we assume that the fiscal burden in New Spain was considerably higher, an eightfold difference necessarily implies that per capita GDP in the domestic economy of New Spain was very high'.[26] This, in turn, casts considerable doubt on the claims of Coatsworth and others that the divergence in economic growth between Spain and Anglo-America began as early as 1700.[27]

The case for a post-1800 divergence is further strengthened by a second conclusion, which is elaborated considerably more than the first. This is that the Spanish Crown, by this point at least, was not extracting revenue from America for use in Europe but was overseeing very substantial transfers from one region to another with the objective of forging an autonomous security community out of the American realms. The first leg of this argument is consistent with earlier

(http://www.nuff.ox.ac.uk/Economics/History/); Regina Grafe and Maria Alejandra Irigoin, 'The Spanish Empire and Its Legacy: Fiscal Re-distribution and Political Conflict in Colonial and Post-Colonial Spanish America,' *Working Papers of the Global Economic History Network* (GEHN) no. 23/06 (2006)(http://www.lse.ac.uk/collections/economichistory/GEHN/Default.htm).

[25] Tulio Halperín Donghi, 'Backward Looks and Forward Glimpses from a Quincentennial Vantage Point,' *Journal of Latin American Studies*, Supplement (1992), p. 221, quoted in Grafe and Irigoin, 'The Spanish Empire,' p. 5.

[26] Grafe and Irigoin, 'The Spanish Empire,' p.19. The dollar and the peso were more or less at parity.

[27] Coatsworth, 'Economic and Institutional Trajectories'.

scholarship, establishing a decline in remittances to Spain of revenue collected in Lima from 64 per cent in the 1590s to levels consistently of ten per cent or less after the 1660s.[28] As for inter-regional transfers, between 1785 and 1800 these seem to have consisted in substantial net flows away from New Spain (today's Mexico) and into the Rio de la Plata area (today's Argentina and Uruguay), where locally raised revenues in a thinly populated zone acting as a bulwark against Portuguese expansion were regularly supplemented by more than 40 per cent.

The conclusion drawn by Grafe and Irigoin is that, while the Spanish empire, like Spain itself, lacked centralized and uniform modern administration, the very substantial commissions accruing to local elites from inter-regional transfers and state procurement and the evident success of a strategically motivated system that secured the empire against external threat for nigh on three hundred years were sufficient to win acquiescence in resource transfers just so long as the Crown continued to legitimate the system and act as final arbiter.

It was this legitimacy that dissolved in the chaos of 1808. In 1807, Napoleon Bonaparte gained permission from his ally, Spain, to move troops through Spain in order to attack Portugal. By December he had taken Lisbon, but had also, in effect, occupied Spain. In March, his country by now host to over 100,000 French troops, Charles IV abdicated in favour of his son, who ascended the throne as Ferdinand VII. Ferdinand, in turn, was forced by pro-reform elements in Spain and the Emperor Napoleon to abdicate just four months later in favour of Joseph Bonaparte, King of Naples and elder brother of the Emperor. Though Ferdinand was restored in 1813 and was to reign for a further twenty years, the prestige of the monarchy had been greatly diminished. Subsequent succession wars contributed to the political and economic stagnation of Spain throughout the nineteenth century and it was not really until after the Bourbon restoration in 1975, following the death of Franco, that a satisfactory reconciliation of monarch and people was undertaken.

The more immediate impact of the events of 1808 was that the fiscal system collapsed, reliant as it had been on the authority of the Crown. As much in Iberia as in America, a squabble for control of revenues and territory ensued that would cause political turmoil and material devastation for more than half a century. In short, far from metropolitan rapacity causing a relative decline in Spanish American economic performance before independence, Grafe and Irigoin see decline as a consequence of the collapse of a relatively successful imperial fiscal regime, of which the principal fault − if fault it can be called − was its integration and sophistication, by comparison with what had existed within the British empire in North America.

---

[28] John J. TePaske, 'New World Silver, Castile, and the Philippines,' cited by Grafe and Irigoin, 'The Spanish Empire,' p. 20.

Scientific Racism

Those arguments for an Anglo-Latin divide that have so far been examined have been attached to quite clear moves in the European dance of Great Power rivalry. Contemporary use of 'Latin' to denote countries in which French, Spanish, Italian or Portuguese are spoken derived from French anxieties of the 1860s about Pan-Slavism and British naval, industrial and imperial pre-eminence. The Black Legend was rooted in Anglo-Spanish rivalries and its Romanticized version was an aspect of the cultural counter-revolution that followed the Napoleonic Wars in Europe. The association of Protestantism with enterprise was linked to the Prussian bid for hegemony within a united Germany. The last two chapters of the story are less European. Originating in Europe, they do not so much sweep, wave-like, across the Atlantic, as root there, like grafts on a new and vigorous stock.

Scientific racism is generally traced to French and English writers of the mid-nineteenth century. It was fed by the work of Arthur Gobineau (1816–1882) in France, whose *Essay on the Inequality of the Human Races* was published in Paris between 1853 and 1855, by a misidentification of linguistic and genetic variation in some of the writings of Oxford professor Friedrich Max Müller (1823–1900) and by rising awareness of the work of Charles Darwin (1809–1882). Researchers busied themselves measuring and drawing in an attempt to identify racial types. Typical of this sort of amateur scholar was John Beddoe (1826–1911), an English physician who journeyed tirelessly through Britain recording the eye and hair colour of populations in different locations and formulating an 'index of nigrescence' from which he drew entirely unjustified conclusions about the sources from which different parts of the country had been populated.[29]

By the end of the nineteenth century scientific racism was widespread, leading a progressive English liberal like J. A. Hobson to drop into his seminal work on imperialism the suggestion that no great European War could break out without the permission of the Rothschilds.[30] But though it must be supposed that the works of Gobineau and his successors were influential in the USA, disagreement over abolition and the larger question of whether Americans of African descent could be integrated into a free society were sufficient to ensure the growth of a home-grown and vigorous school of scientific racism there.

Nor was Latin America immune. Long used to a complex set of distinctions between castes, complete with vocabulary and emblems, Latin Americans had lived in a highly-racialized society since the Conquest. Yet European writings of

---

[29] For a recent and sympathetic portrait, see Bryan Sykes, *Blood of the Isles: Exploring the Genetic Roots of our Tribal History* (London, 2006).

[30] J.A. Hobson, *Imperialism: A Study* [1902] (London, 3rd, ed. 1938), p. 57.

the mid-nineteenth century provided fresh resources for new forms of racism. Argentine liberals of the Generation of 1837 were almost uniformly racist, Juan Batista Alberdi (1810–1884) remarking that '[i]n America everything that is not European is barbarous' while Domingo Faustino Sarmiento (1811–1888) insisted that indigenous Americans were the detritus of 'a prehistoric, servile race'. Members of the South American elites would no more have expected to meet with racial discrimination themselves in Europe or the United States than Ghandi, coming from British India, would have expected the treatment he received in South Africa or a Vietnamese Party official would have expected to encounter prejudice in 1980s Moscow. Yet, as the new racism fused with the old, this was precisely what they would meet with, and what would obscure the cultural community of American elites and bedevil their persistent attempts at cooperation.

At the very moment when Hispanic-American social elites were gladly tearing off the wrappings of a new Latin identity, fresh from Paris, thinking to mark themselves off from the indigenous and mixed-race masses they ruled, Europe and the USA were moving remorselessly toward an all-embracing and hierarchical taxonomy which would rudely knock the Spanish speakers off the winners' podium.

The New Imperialism

The final and decisive force operating against a continental vision of the Western hemisphere in the twentieth century was more overtly political and American than those considered thus far, though still a reaction to Old World power politics. The last third of the century was the period during which the United States of America, recovering from the catastrophic civil war which many had thought would put paid to it, broke loose from its moorings and irrevocably set a course for overseas empire. Until the future of the Union had been settled, implosion and disintegration remained possible. English novelist Anthony Trollope could nevertheless reflect, during the early months of the Civil War, upon the astonishment with which George Washington would surely have responded to the extraordinary progress of his nation had he lived to 1860. 'He did not dream of the speedy addition to his already gathered constellations of those western states, of Wisconsin, Illinois, Minnesota, and Iowa; nor did he dream of Texas conquered, Louisiana purchased, and Missouri and Kansas rescued from the wilderness.' Still less did Trollope and his contemporaries, convinced as so many of them were of the inevitability of secession, dream of a strong federal government.

It is of course possible to argue for an earlier moment of no return. In European geopolitical terms, the time to have checked the United States would almost certainly have been the 1840s. Though he recognised a unifying national character as he travelled through the United States, it is evident that the United States was not yet a single country for Trollope, as is clear from his repeated treatment of 'the United States' as a plural grammatical subject.[31] Flanked by autonomous sovereign states in Texas and California, as well as by Canada, Mexico and a still-Russian Alaska, the federal government might have suffered interventions in its Civil War and subsequent campaigns against the remaining indigenous polities of the Western plains, or else have been deterred from embarking on such conflicts. This in turn might have constrained its territorial extension and economic growth with incalculable results. But Texan independence was fleeting (1836–45), annexation of California in 1848 forestalled the emergence of an independent republic on the West Coast, condominium with the British in Oregon was ended in 1846, while Mexico was roundly defeated the same year and vast tracts of its territory annexed.

After 1850, with all of these issues resolved in favour of the USA, the prospect of intrusion of European geopolitical machinations into the Western hemisphere pretty much dissolved into fantasy, notwithstanding the modest size of the armed forces of the Union.[32] European powers did not intervene in the US Civil War; Alaska was quietly purchased from Russia in 1867; a self-governing Canada turned inwards to undertake the daunting task of linking the widely dispersed and culturally divergent colonies from which it had been formed; and the absurdity of power balancing in North America was finally demonstrated by the tragicomic French attempt, in 1862–3, to establish a second Mexican Empire governed by a Habsburg prince.

Besides, to construe the events of the 1840s as a lost opportunity to balance the rising power of the USA, as I will later argue at greater length, is not simply nostalgic but misleadingly redolent of Old World perspectives having little to do with American understandings and motivations at the time. In short, while a

---

[31]   Anthony Trollope, *North America*, pp. 209 and 213. '[T]he United States *have* had no outlying colonies or dependencies. . .' and 'I have ever admired the United States as a nation. I have ever admired *their* liberty, *their* prowess. . .' [my emphasis]. Dunkerley notes that 'prior to 1865 the term [United States] was used more in the plural than in the singular. . .' James Dunkerley, *Americana: The Americas in the World around 1850* (London, 2000), p. 27.

[32]   On the eve of the Civil War, in 1860, there were about 16,000 men in the United States army. During the conflict, both sides created large armies, and more than a million were in the field. By 1875, the Federal army had been reduced to 25,000. (6 November 2006) (http://www.spartacus.schoolnet.co.uk/USAarmy.htm).

handful of percipient commentators had already put their money on the United States as an emerging Great Power, the fact of an extensive Anglophone state capable of waging modern warfare with the support of an advanced industrial economy was not fully evident until the extraordinary levels of mobilization seen in the Civil War had been shown to be replicable – mass immigration notwithstanding – through the Spanish-American War and United States intervention in the Great War of 1914–1918.

What triggered United States expansion beyond the continental land mass, however, was less the persistence of residual European possessions in the Americas than the so-called New Imperialism of the last quarter of the nineteenth century, which saw newly acquisitive Britain, France and an eager but lagging German Empire carve up much of Africa and South-East Asia, whilst nibbling voraciously at East Asia and the Pacific. Far from alone among American states in its alarmed response to European annexations, the United States was uniquely capable of response. This was not entirely a matter of wealth. Brazil, Chile, and Argentina were all buyers of the most advanced weapons systems of the time. But they could not build them in their own shipyards, as the United States now could, nor could they match the USA in sheer numbers of battleships and cruisers.[33] Mexico, had it wished to, could hardly have challenged Spain without waking the sleeping monster to its north. This left the United States uniquely well placed to strip Spain of her remaining American dependencies and take on the role of self-appointed policeman in the Greater Caribbean.

This birth of United States imperialism is open to at least four interpretations. It may be seen, rather as Iberian expansion is sometimes seen, as a spilling over of the forces that had only recently completed conquest of the homeland. It might be construed as the consequence of a failure of balancing resulting from the neglect of a Europe distracted by war, fear of revolution and the prospects of easy pickings in Africa and Asia. It might even, like that of Japan, be seen primarily as an imitative reaction to the unintended yet implicit threat posed by British, French and German aggressions elsewhere. (If you wish to stand among them, don't do as the Great Powers say; do as they do.[34]) But there is also one last way of viewing the matter. It might be thought a consequence of the emerging sense of difference and superiority that has been traced here: the liberating mission of a country that cannot be imperialist because it has itself been in bondage to Old Europe and fought for its own emancipation.

---

[33] Thomas Brassey, *Naval Annual* (Portsmouth, 1886 –).

[34] Shogo Suzuki, 'Japan's Socialization into Janus-faced European International Society,' *European Journal of International Relations*, vol. 11, no. 1 (March 2005), pp. 137–64.

Conclusion

Explaining why the distinction between the USA and Latin America has seemed so natural over the past century has turned out to be a complicated matter. But all six strands of the explanation have one thing in common. They are rooted in power politics, and generally in the power plays of Old Europe. The very word 'Latin,' that has been used since the 1880s to label Spanish and Portuguese speaking America, was coined by French propagandists as they squared up against Britain and France in the third quarter of the nineteenth century. The Black Legend was developed by English propagandists during two long centuries of intermittent warfare with Spain. Its nineteenth-century romanticization was in part a response to Catholic migrations in the nineteenth century. These, in their turn, were partly economic but also reflected oppressive systems of labour and land tenure in Italy, Ireland and elsewhere. And indeed, the Romantic movement within which Cooper, Irving and the New England historians positioned themselves was in some measure a conservative response to the French Revolution and the challenges it had mounted to hereditary privilege and faith. The Protestant work ethic turns out to have been implicated in highly contestable Prussian claims about the centrality of Protestantism in German national identity. Scientific racism was taken up with alacrity by European publics in the later nineteenth century as a way of justifying racial panic when country folk, often distinguished by religion, language, dress and diet, were pouring into industrializing cities, while marked cultural difference was being incorporated into the metropolis (Ireland united with Britain in 1800; Algeria incorporated into France in 1848), and improved transport and communications exposed more and more West European women to the prospects of miscegenation or even capture on imperial frontiers. In the United States it had far more to do with the predicament of southern elites, struggling to re-impose and vindicate white supremacy as the reconstruction era drew to a close. The discourse of the Monroe Doctrine and of the USA as post-colonial and anti-imperialist state, liberating Spain's last American dependencies, may also be attributed to power politics as, firstly, neither the European powers nor the larger American states managed to balance effectively against a rapidly expanding United States and, from 1880, the Europeans failed adequately to reassure the USA that their 'New Imperialism' posed no threat to the hemisphere.

The common-sense view, that the United States and Latin America are worlds apart, turns out to have arisen pretty much in the half-century between 1840 and 1890 and to have rested on a series of propagandist claims, many of them European. To discover how this came about and to appreciate the ways in which recent historiographic revisions have eaten away at long-established beliefs about the political character of the Reformation or the fiscal system of the Spanish empire is to realise how far from natural or obvious it is to mark off the United States from the rest of the continent and how odd to link it with Europe in a supposedly homogeneous Western civilization. However this merely opens the door. The argument so far has been negative. It is now time to ask what reason there may be to think of the USA and its neighbours as a group with positive features in common and an international society distinct from that of Europe? What marks off the Americas, and only the Americas?

CHAPTER II

A Common American History

The idea of Latin America as a region distinct from and generally subordinate to the United States was naturalized at the very moment when the southern republics finally got themselves organized and set about embracing modernity wholeheartedly. To put it another way, the perception of a divided hemisphere was established just at the very moment when comparative and hemispheric approaches to American history might have been most appropriate and fruitful.

Awareness of the historical contingency of this conceptual division of the hemisphere and its roots in international politics sets one free to undertake the thought experiment of a continental American history. Many have attempted this, but their work has done little to undo the damage, and the notion of a common American history has had little impact in the United States over the past hundred years.

The work of Herbert Bolton stands out among the first attempts.[35] Bolton argued that students of history in his country ought to begin with an outline course of American history before engaging in more specific study of its component parts. By America, he meant the whole continent. He justified this in part by drawing an analogy with Europe. But the fact is that the close texture of their ruling dynasties, the operations of the balance of power, and high levels of economic interdependence made Europe a single commonwealth, as Burke would have put it, or, in modern parlance, an international *society* as distinct from

---

[35] Herbert Eugene Bolton, 'The Epic of Greater America,' *American Historical Review*, vol. 38, no. 3 (April 1933), pp. 448–74, is reprinted with some anticipations of his view and several critiques and responses in Lewis Hanke (ed.), *Do the Americas Have a Common History – A Critique of the Bolton Theory* (New York, 1964). See also Herbert Heaton, 'Other Wests than Ours,' *Journal of Economic History*, vol. 6 (supplement 1946), pp. 50–62. My references to Bolton use the pagination of Hanke's collection.

a mere *system* of states. By contrast, interactions in the Americas were initially derivative of the European balance and later far less intensive than those in Europe. It is a matter of degree, of course. They merit study but do not clearly constitute a context without which the histories of any individual colony or group of colonies were unintelligible much before the nineteenth century.

If one facet of the problem of American history has been lack of an entirely convincing hemispheric periodization and narrative, a second – of equal importance – has been neglect of the many opportunities that there have been to make much more specific comparisons, since these might have prompted the kinds of conjectures and research projects that could have developed such a historiography, bottom up, until the processes of accumulation and attrition yielded a broader and more robust conception of the hemisphere as a whole. Some of these will be touched upon as the argument unfolds. How odd it is, for example, that recent revisionist work on United States military culture has proceeded as though oblivious to ways in which it has been closing the gap between US ways of war and those of other American states, while distancing both from Europe.[36] How odd, again, that US historians have generally dealt with populism, religiosity, racism and corruption as domestic rather than continental issues in spite of the fact that many of these supposedly distinctive features can be observed elsewhere, leading one recent historian to insist that 'American history must be studied comparatively'.[37]

Bolton must carry some responsibility for this, since a second weakness of his thesis was its chronological form. In the celebrated 1932 Toronto address as President of the American Historical Association, he had emphasized successive broad phases into which continental history could be divided and his primary thesis appeared to be the possibility of a single hemispheric narrative covering discovery, settlement, European rivalries, independence, consolidation and state-building – an account culminating, one suspects, in continental cooperation. The trouble with such an approach was that it lay wide open to Edmundo O'Gorman's criticisms of superficiality and materialism unless it addressed the question of culture. If one were concerned simply with economic history it would make far more sense to group together for comparative study the set of more or less temperate lands of extensive European settlement, including Australia, New Zealand, Canada, Siberia, Argentina, Uruguay, Southern Brazil and, for a time, South Africa. Such was the plan, in Bolton's generation, proposed

---

[36]   John Grenier, *The First Way of War: American War Making on the Frontier* (Cambridge, 2005); Fred Anderson and Andrew Cayton, *The Dominion of War: Empire and Conflict in America, 1500–2000* (London, 2005).

[37]   C.A. Bayly, *The Birth of the Modern World, 1780–1914: Global Connections and Comparisons* (Oxford, 2004), p. 470.

by Herbert Heaton, though Latin America was largely forgotten in the main body of the paper.[38] Such was the context of much of my own early work.[39] But while this might yield explanation it would not generate understanding.

Only at the very end of his address, and in a very few words, did Bolton began to anticipate this criticism by identifying *themes* to which the continental narrative would direct research, and which promised to delve more deeply into the roots of American culture and justify a hemispheric approach. His list included the study of borderlands, the introduction and spread of new species, industrial and commercial activity, mining, missions, policies toward First Nations, slavery and emancipation, constitutional development and forms of conflict resolution: still, it may be objected, a plausible check-list for the history of lands of European settlement in general rather than of the Americas, specifically.

It was left to Bolton's successors to refine this list of topics in a more dialectical and specifically American manner. Philip Brooks, for example, produced his own excellent list: conquest of the land, miscegenation and the continuing tension between independence and European culture, tensions between mercantilism and economic liberalism, and religiosity or − as he put it − 'the strong bond of Christianity throughout the hemisphere'.[40] George W. Brown, writing in a 1942 retrospect of Bolton's thesis, went further by insisting that seeming contradictions were quintessentially American. Elaborating on his view that Canada was 'never more American' than when she declared war in September 1939, he affirmed that '[a]lways . . . running through American history, there have been the contradictory elements of separation from, and association with, Europe. Canada's paradox of autonomy and co-operation is not un-American; it is the American experience in a unique form'.[41]

Later examples of historical thought about the hemisphere as a whole abound. They include Edmundo O'Gorman's entirely justified use of what was before long to become a hackneyed form of title in *The Invention of America*, Alistair Hennessy's expansion of Turner's frontier thesis to the continent as a whole, Richard W. Slatta's related work on cowboys, *gauchos* and *llaneros*, my own

---

[38]   Herbert Heaton, 'Other Wests Than Ours,' *Journal of Economic History*, vol. 6, no. 1 (May 1946), pp. 50–62.

[39]   Charles A. Jones, 'The Fiscal Motive for Monetary and Banking Legislation in Argentina, Australia and Canada before 1914,' in D. C. M. Platt and Guido di Tella (eds.), *Argentina, Australia and Canada: Studies in Comparative Development, 1870–1965* (London &c, 1985), pp. 123–38.

[40]   Philip C. Brooks, 'Do the Americas Share a Common History?' *Revista de Historia de América*, no. 33 (1952), pp. 75–83, reprinted in part in Hanke, *Do the Americas Have a Common History*, pp. 134–40.

[41]   George W. Brown, 'A Canadian View,' *Canadian Historical Review* vol. 23 (1942), pp. 132–38, reprinted in part in Hanke.

attempt to think in one breath about economic relations between Britain and the whole of the Americas since independence, broader treatments of the sort offered by Felipe Fernández-Arnesto or Lester D. Langley and – still more broadly – literatures dealing with ethno-history and environmental history which ride roughshod over imposed frontiers.[42]

Notwithstanding all this, it is hard to dissent from Alistair Hennessy's judgment, three decades ago, that Bolton's appeal has gone 'largely unheeded,' while even some of those who *have* accepted the challenge of regarding the hemisphere as a whole may plead guilty to the charge levelled by Felipe Fernández-Arnesto that, when contemplating the history of the Americas, 'conscious as we are of the might and magnetism of the United States today . . . we underestimate the contribution of the rest of the hemisphere. . .'[43] Yet it is with the Bolton tradition, in its thematic, dialectical, even contrary variant, that this book identifies.

Religiosity

What, then, might be the agenda of an American history? Drawing on a distinction made half a century ago by Geoffrey Barraclough, this question will be approached in two discrete yet ultimately convergent ways. Contemporary history, Barraclough explained, was the process by which the present interrogated the past for explanations of current problems. Modern history, by contrast, traced the working through of a great historical transformation, modernity, the inception of which used to be located quite precisely in 1453, when Christian Constantinople (present-day Istanbul) fell to the Ottoman Turks. It takes only a moment to realize that contemporary history may range further in time and space than modern history, reaching back to the creation of religious, linguistic or political frontiers or to decisive battles hundreds of years ago to explain events today. Modern history is a much less open process. It need not accept the old conventional starting date, but once *some* starting date has been selected, its spatial limits and its forward direction are largely set.[44]

---

[42] Edmundo O'Gorman, *The Invention of America: An Inquiry into the Historical Nature of the New World and the Meaning of its History* (Bloomington IN, 1961) and (in opposition to Bolton) 'Do the Americas Have a Common History?' *Points of View*, no. 3 (Washington, 1941), pp. 1–10, reprinted in Hanke, pp. 103–111; Alistair Hennessy, *The Frontier in Latin American History* (Albuquerque, 1978); Richard W. Slatta, *Comparing Cowboys and Frontiers* (Norman and London, 1997); Charles A. Jones, *El reino unido y américa: inversiones e influencia económica* (Madrid, 1992); Felipe Fernández-Arnesto, *The Americas: the History of a Hemisphere* (London, 2003); Lester D. Langley, *The Americas in the Modern Age* (New Haven and London, 2003).

[43] Hennessy, *The Frontier*, p. 2; Fernández-Arnesto, *The Americas*, p. 61.

[44] Geoffrey Barraclough, *Introduction to Contemporary History* (Harmondsworth, 1967), pp. 1–35.

Three features of contemporary America that may serve as starting point for a contemporary history: religiosity, ethnic diversity and violent crime. The first is especially interesting because it was recently deployed by Samuel Huntington as part of his answer to the eponymous question he had addressed to his compatriots: Who Are We?[45] Huntington set out to show that one of the most salient features of the USA was the abiding and intense religiosity of its people. By this is meant not just their nominal affiliation to some church or other, but the strength of their religious convictions as measured by formal membership of religious organizations, disdain for atheists, belief in the literal truth of the Bible, and answers to survey questions about frequency of prayer and the centrality of religion in their lives. Not only are those who live in the USA unusually religious, they are also notably more religious than Europeans and much more religious than one would expect in so rich a country. How is this to be explained? Does it, as Huntington believes, help constitute and explain the exceptionalism of the USA?

It used to be widely assumed that the fruit of a modernity rooted in reason would be secularism. In Victorian England textual scholarship and advances in the natural sciences upset literal interpretation of the Bible and Radicals who had campaigned against slavery and for free trade also attacked the finances of the established Anglican Church by challenging tithes in the courts. In France positivism was developed by Henri de Saint Simon and others as something close to a secular church. Freemasonry flourished throughout Europe and beyond.

This challenge to traditional religious authority did not go unopposed. A dominant aspect of the Romantic movement which swept Europe in the immediate aftermath of Napoleon's defeat was its underpinning of the restoration of monarchy and church through a revival of interest in medieval life, including religious practice and experience. This, coupled with a sensibility that married individualism to apprehension of the sublime, made Romanticism a powerful ally of reaction and religious revivalism. Yet steady scientific and technological advance, the move of European populations to the cities, the advance of literacy and mass print media and the cultivation of nationalism as quasi-religion all forced organized religion on to the back foot throughout Europe.

There it remained until the 1960s, surely the apogee of secularism, after which a number of contrary tendencies gathered strength. Religion had helped fuel political dissidence in countries as disparate as the African colonies of the European powers and the European satellites of the Soviet Union. Whether it was the experience of organization and responsibility gained by leaders of independent churches or the spiritual strength that came from surreptitious devotion in the Orthodox world or the way the two were conjoined in the Estonian

---

[45]   Huntington, *Who Are We?*

choral movement, religion began to rekindle more widely and more fiercely in the 1970s, evident in the opposition of Catholic Poland and Moslem Afghanistan to Russia by the end of the decade and gradually igniting challenges to the secular state in countries as disparate as Turkey, India, China, France and the USA itself.

Although widespread, this revival of religiosity has not been uniform, nor has its effect on the secular state been uniformly corrosive. There are marked disparities between the USA and Europe regarding levels of religious belief and practice. Moreover, it is not so much religiosity as the combination of wealth, religiosity and a secular state that forms one of the most interesting and plausible strands of arguments for US exceptionalism: the idea that the purpose of the secular state has been to marginalize or even suppress Christianity in Europe while, in the USA, it has been to facilitate it. The Founding Fathers, it may fairly be said, pioneered the path later to be followed with less enduring success by Kemal Atatürk in Turkey and Jawaharlal Nehru in India, a country which has a plausible claim to have originated the secular state centuries ago. Nothing was further from their minds than the suppression of faith; they realized that without a secular state religious difference could tear communities apart.

Concerned to stress this aspect of United States exceptionalism, Huntington drew on reports of a 1991 survey of religious belief in seventeen countries which placed the USA clearly in the lead, with a score of 1.7 as compared to the 8.3 of Jewish Israel, the 10.6 of Catholic Austria and the 11.6 of a nominally Anglican UK.[46] What he did not say is that the USA was the only American country in the sample. From another source, he lists no less than forty-two countries, ranked by declared levels of religiosity. Nigeria led with a score over 90 per cent. Poland, in the grip of a resurgent and Anti-Communist Catholicism at the time the survey was conducted, came second. The United States, in fifth place, with a score around 66 per cent, scored higher than Brazil, Chile, Mexico, Argentina and Canada, which clustered between 50 per cent and 65 per cent. What is interesting is that these American countries all scored higher than most major West European countries, with West Germany and Spain in the 40s and France and Britain in the 30s.

The results of a recent Gallup survey of declarations of religious faith are summarised in Table 2.1. Aggregation blunts the figures in several ways. Religiosity differs from one country to another and, within each country, by income, level of education, sex, region and ethnic group. What really marks out the United States is that it is by far the most religious of the world's *wealthiest* countries. The

---

[46]   Huntington, *Who Are We?* p. 90, citing George Bishop, 'What Americans Really believe and Why Faith Isn't As Universal as They Think,' *Free Inquiry* (Summer, 1999), pp. 38–42.

Table 2.1   Declarations of Religious Faith or Atheism by Region

	Percentage claiming to be religious	*Percentage claiming to be convinced atheists*
North America	71	1
Western Europe	60	9
Latin America	71	1
Africa	91	1
Asia Pacific	65	12
East and Central Europe	65	4

Source: Gallop International, 'Voice of the People 2005: Religiosity around the world'. These figures summarize results of a survey carried out in 65 countries between May and July 2005. The figures for the Middle East appear to have been based on a highly unrepresentative sample and have been omitted.

Pew Global Attitudes Project, surveying 44 countries in 2002, found that 59 per cent of people questioned in the United States said that religion played a very important part in their lives, as compared with 30 per cent in Canada, 11 per cent in France, 12 per cent in Japan. (Britain, in this as in so many aspects of life, was closest to the USA of the European countries surveyed, with 33 per cent compared with traditionally pious Italy's 27 per cent.)[47] An earlier poll, in 1999, cited by Huntington, found that 86 per cent of those living in the USA believed in God.[48] Nor is this religiosity of recent date. It has been a consistent feature of Anglophone North America from the start. As de Tocqueville remarked: 'Religion, which, among Americans, never mixes directly in the government of society, should therefore be considered the first of their political institutions, for if it does not give them the taste for freedom, it singularly facilitates their use of it.'[49] Huntington goes further, arguing effectively for the persistence of Christianity in spite of the immigration of non-Christian groups. He points to the steady decline of Judaism in the USA from four per cent in the 1920s to two per cent by the late 1990s and to the predominance of Christian belief among immigrants not only from Latin America but also from East Asia.[50]

---

[47]   Pew Global Attitudes Project. Press release: December 19, 2002. 'Among wealthy nations . . . the U.S. stands alone in its embrace of religion.' (http://www.pewglobal.org).
[48]   Huntington, *Who Are We?* p. 86, citing Gallup/CNN/*USA Today* poll, 9–12 December 1999.
[49]   Alexis de Tocqueville, *Democracy in America* (Chicago IL, 2000), p. 280. Huntington quotes de Tocqueville to much the same effect, *Who Are We?* p. 85.
[50]   Huntington, *Who Are We?* p. 100.

It is remarkable that Huntington, in his treatment of religiosity, should draw such a strong contrast between the USA and secular Europe, yet not comment on the very similar levels of religiosity prevailing throughout the Americas. Yet it might be claimed that these mean very little, firstly because it is not religiosity *per se* but the combination of wealth and religiosity that is remarkable in the USA and second because the distinction between Catholic Latin America and a predominantly Protestant USA vitiates any comparison.

To the first of these objections one reply must be that the correlation at work in the USA may be less between wealth and religiosity than between inequality and religiosity. Of the major Latin American countries included in the Pew survey it is Brazil – economically the most successful over the past generation yet still marked by pronounced inequalities of income and wealth – that stands out as the most religious, with 77 per cent of respondents claiming that religion plays a very important part in their lives. The figure for Argentina, by contrast, was 39 per cent. It is therefore significant that Gini coefficients (used as a measure of income inequality) for the USA and Brazil have in recent decades been in the range 0.4–0.45 and 0.6–0.65 respectively, while those for the UK and Argentina have ranged between 0.25–0.35 and 0.25–0.4.[51] In short, of each of the two pairs of countries – the USA and the UK; Brazil and Argentina – it has been the one with less income equality that has proved the more religious.

The force of the second objection, that the predominantly Catholic religiosity of Latin America and the Protestantism of the United States make their similar levels of religiosity merely coincidental, runs into three problems. The most obvious is that Protestantism has been making tremendous inroads into the Catholic South in recent decades, while Latin American inward migration has boosted Catholicism to some degree within the United States. But it should also be born in mind that the distinction between Catholicism was traditionally overdrawn in the Americas because of its close alignment with political and military rivalries. Recent historiography, surveyed in chapter 1, has cast doubt on the Black Legend in its various forms as, also, upon Max Weber's association of economic advance and industrialization with Protestantism. The tendency, noted by Huntington, for even Roman Catholicism to speak with an American accent in the New World was anticipated, from the sixteenth century, by the pan-European phenomenon of confessionalism, as a convergence of structure and political function between national churches, whether Protestant or Roman, took place beneath the skin of doctrinal dissent.

---

[51] United Nations University World Institute for Development Economics Research (http://www.wider.unn.edu/wiid/wiid.htm).

Ethnicity

A second area of acute political concern in the United States today is ethnic diversity. Indeed, it was the central theme of Huntington's 2004 book. The nub of his argument is expressed with characteristic bluntness in his concluding pages. 'Americans' – he writes – 'can embrace the world, that is, open their country to other peoples and cultures, or they can try to reshape those other peoples and cultures in terms of American values, or they can maintain their society and culture distinct from those of other peoples.'[52] What is to be the place of the USA in the world, Huntington asks: cosmopolitan, imperial or national? The answer he provides is a rejection of cosmopolitan liberalism and neo-conservatism imperialism in favour of a socially conservative and isolationist nationalism. The answer I offer, with the trepidation that must accompany any intervention in the affairs of another nation, is that, while there is much to be said for the negative elements of Huntington's argument, his excessive and unjustified emphasis on US exceptionalism obscures the extent to which his country, by reaching a new understanding of its place in the hemisphere, might rein in the least responsible aspects of liberal and neoconservative policy and adopt a more balanced posture toward the wider world.

For the time being, however, it is one rather narrower aspect of Huntington's argument that demands attention. This is the supposed danger arising from Mexican immigration. Huntington claims that immigrants from elsewhere in the continent, but from Mexico above all, are now so numerous as to form enclaves within the USA that do not share in its political culture and pose problems of integration that are unprecedented and may prove insurmountable. In the past, immigrants came from far away and lacked cheap transport and communications. Contact with the homeland was difficult; participation in its political affairs virtually impossible. Overcoming barriers of language and culture might take a generation, but adoption of the American way of life together with escape from the ghetto through education and sheer hard work were the focus of life for millions of Irish, German and Italian immigrants during the century up to the 1960s. The new immigrants come from settlements in nearby countries. They can easily maintain contact with the communities in which they grew up by telephone and relatively frequent visits. In large urban centres in the USA it is easy for them pretty much to avoid the need to speak English. They have their own print and broadcast media. In those cases where the constitution allows they are courted by the politicians of their countries of origin. Why should they ever adopt the American creed?

---

[52] Huntington, *Who Are We?* p. 363.

Huntington's argument provoked an internet frenzy, as members of Mexican-American business associations and other community leaders pointed in perfect English to the successes of integration and the commitment of immigrants to that central pillar of the American creed, hard work. But all this is to miss the point entirely. In drawing attention to the mote of Mexican immigration, Huntington has forgotten the beam of an African-American population that has still not entirely succeeded in integrating into its homeland almost a century and a half after the abolition of slavery. Once again, as with religiosity, he has not noticed that if the Americas are viewed as a whole and compared with Western Europe, it is the existence and durability of communities (not everywhere minorities) that are inassimilable that stands out as typical of the Americas as a whole. No racist in his heart or in the words on the page, Huntington has nevertheless been accused of racism, and the charge is justified to this extent: that he failed to observe that the critical determinant of non-assimilation in the Americas has been the racialization of minorities. Ethnic and linguistic differences may be overcome. In this sense Argentina, Brazil, Canada and the USA have all been relatively successful melting pots. But wherever cultural difference has been construed in racial terms assimilation has proven elusive.

This is a minefield. The variability of ethnic or quasi-ethnic categories employed in national censuses and the differing incentives to identify with one group or another mean that there is precious little chance of constructing a neat table analysing the population of each American republic by ethnic group in a consistent and politically acceptable way. There is still disagreement about the extent to which race is anything more than a social construct, about the relationship between race and skin colour, and about the distinction between ethnicity and race. *The World Bank Atlas*, a slim volume that maps poverty, infant life chances, education, disease, gender, water, forests, energy, investment, trade and debt, does not attempt to deal with ethnicity or race.[53]

Works that do try to tackle the problem often suffer from what had better be termed 'the American problem'. Since it will crop up again before we are done this had better be spelt out. I have in mind the commonsense reference, un-picked a little in chapter 1, to the USA as America, and the consequent paucity of analyses that cover the continent as a whole. An 'Atlas of American Society', for example, covers only the United States.[54] A reference handbook on world population gives aggregate figures for Europe, Oceania, Asia and Africa, but not America. Instead, the aggregates are for North America (which excludes

---

[53] *World Bank Atlas* (Washington DC, 2004).
[54] Alice C. Andrews and James W. Fonseca, *The Atlas of American Society* (New York and London, 1995).

Mexico) and Latin America and the Caribbean. It is silent on the question of systematic treatments of ethnicity.[55] A school atlas attempts the impossible, assuring readers that its factfile 'has been researched from the most up-to-date and authoritative sources', and ends up with egg all over its face, accepting as ethnic categories (presumably from government statistical offices) incommensurable terms as variable as Welsh, Indo-European, White, Jewish, Quechua and Hispanic. Sometimes skin colour is used, sometimes language, sometimes religion and sometimes mere residence. (A great many non-Catalans live in Catalonia; a great many Scots in England, but the figures given appear to be for residents in the two countries, not those identifying as Catalans or Scots.) Use of 'mixed-race' and '*mestizo*', undefined, throws more spanners into the works. It seems there are no blacks or African-Americans in Colombia, but there are, one is relieved to read, 22 per cent 'other'. Elsewhere, as little as one per cent gives you your own column (Native Americans in the USA; Roma in Spain). In the United States, the talk is all of where people came from (African-American, Italian-American, etc.). In Brazil, hyphenation gives way to skin colour which, to a greater extent than in the USA, can be changed by education, dress and wealth. Memorably, the president of the USA asks the president of Brazil, 'Do you have blacks too?'[56]

Is any generalization possible? I believe so. Most American republics have, and have had for much longer than the states of Western Europe, very substantial socially marginalized and racialized groups in their midst: African-Americans in Colombia, Brazil and the United States; people of indigenous descent in the Andean countries and Mexico.[57] The history of these groups since independence has been distinct from that of European immigrant groups defined by language or nation of origin. For all their initial sufferings, European immigrants were seen as the solution to a lack of skilled labour and the vulnerability of unsettled lands; those of African and indigenous origin more often as a problem.[58] The objective of government was to integrate the first group while infantilizing or feminizing the second.

The consequence has been a separation from the mainstream of national life that has fomented the development of distinctive cultures in many parts of the

[55] Geoffrey Gilbert, *World Population: A Reference Handbook* (Santa Barbara CA, 2001).

[56] Edward E. Telles, *Race in Another America: the Significance of Skin Color in Brazil* (Princeton and Oxford, 2004), p. 1, citing *Harper's* (June 2002).

[57] Notable exceptions include the racialization at various times of the Roma and European Jewry and of the Irish by English and Scots colonists.

[58] Winthrop Jordan, *White Over Black: American Attitudes toward the Negro, 1550–1812* (Baltimore, 1971).

Americas, characterised by syncretic forms of worship, musical styles and dress-styles. There comes a point when emancipation can hardly be achieved without sacrificing those very badges of resistance which have come, by historic irony, to play a part in their own continued subjection. Even in Mexico and Brazil, where very different attempts have been made to base national identity in a *mestizo* or 'mixed-race' personal identity or in the formula of 'racial democracy', the terms of debate have generally been set by creole elites. Moreover, the republican project in post-independence America did not admit of any continuation of the early-modern solution to this issue, which had been sought in distinctive relations between indigenous people and the Crown, whether of England, Spain or France.

Indeed, if one were asked to identify the central theme of the modern history of America and other zones of sustained creole rule such as New Zealand, Australia and, until lately, South Africa and Zimbabwe, might it not be the implanting of liberal republicanism in racialized societies?[59] And as for the principal stumbling block in the path of this project, it must surely be the incompatibility of sustained social exclusion and democratic institutions. President Thabo Mbeke was not being entirely fanciful when he suggested, during the 2006 visit of Evo Morales, president elect of Bolivia at the time, that Bolivia was following in the footsteps that had led to the end of white rule in South Africa. Nor is it any small thing that it was to take a century of further repression after abolition before the freed slaves of the United States would be in a position to begin a struggle for civil and political rights that is not yet won.

Social Violence

These racial struggles invite discussion of a third feature of contemporary America, alongside religiosity and the racialization of cultural difference, that links North and South and marks off both from the Old World. The Americas today have higher homicide rates than Western Europe. Why should this be? What, if any, is its connection with religiosity and racism?

Once again this is a familiar theme in discussion of the USA. The universal popularity of United States cinema and television programmes has for decades projected the image of a society in which violent crime is endemic, most of all in

---

[59]   I am fully aware that in extending the term creole to all descendents of European settlers I am removing the usual geographical restriction; inclusion of Australasia in the New World, though clearly not in America, has precedents, and is to be preferred to the cumbersome and less than entirely accurate phrase 'temperate lands of European settlement' that is sometimes used to group the principal former British Dominions (and set them aside from other settler states).

Table 2.2. Homicides per 100,000 and Rankings in Selected
Latin American Countries

	UN Rank (World)	PAHO Rank (Latin America)	IADB Rank (Latin America)	UN Rate per 100,000	PAHO Rate per 100,000	IADB Rate per 100,000
Colombia	1	1	3	62	69	90
Jamaica	3	18	4	32	1	35
Dominican Republic	28	4	9	3	4	12
Guatemala	–	17	2	–	1	150

Source: Seventh United Nations Survey of Crime Trends and Operations of Criminal Justice Systems, 1998–2002 (United Nations Office on Drugs and Crime, Centre for International Crime Prevention) as reported by NationMaster at http://www.nationmaster.com; Pan-American Health Organisation (1997) and Inter-American development Bank (2000) as reported by Chaowarit Chaowsangrat, 'Comparative Trends in Violent Crime: the Latin American Context' (accessed at http://www.cerac.org.co).

the inner cities. Once again, as with ethnicity, we encounter an area where not only this disproportionate representation of the US in mass media but also the great differences in national statistics make generalization difficult. One source warns that 'crime statistics are often better indicators of law enforcement and willingness to report crime, than actual prevalence.'[60] There is also considerable variability from one source to another, with the UN Survey of Crime Trends, the Pan-American Health Organisation (PAHO) and the Inter-American Development Bank (IADB) offering widely varying rates and rankings, of which a few of the more extreme are listed in table 2.2. These suggest that some organizations include in their homicide figures, while others exclude, deaths arising from certain forms of social violence, for example homicides by agencies of the state.

It is possible, then, that a combination of over-enthusiastic media and diligent law enforcement has pushed the United States further up the league tables of violent crime than it should be and introduced other significant distortions. This said, with a murder rate of 43 per 100,000, the USA ranks 24th, while the UK, Italy, Spain and Germany rank 46th, 47th, 48th and 49th respectively, with rates

[60] http://www.nationmaster.com/red/graph/cri_mur_percap-crime-murders-per-capit&i. . . 06/12/2006. This internet source relies on the *Seventh United Nations Survey of Crime Trends and Operations of Criminal Justice Systems, 1998–2002* (United Nations Office on Drugs and Crime, Centre for International Crime Prevention).

between 14 and 12. Is this, then, a field in which the Americas as a whole may be contrasted with Western Europe? As with the USA, so with Latin America: the evidence is not clear. Colombia tops the murder rate rankings with Jamaica and Venezuela close behind in third and fourth place. It is tempting to ascribe the relatively high positions of Costa Rica (19) and Uruguay (22), which general reputation might have placed much lower, to high levels of reporting. The absence of Brazil from the top 60 is surprising, given recent press coverage of urban violence, and a cynic might ask whether homicides committed by the authorities are, as in several countries, excluded from the statistics. Regarding violent crime in general, Mauricio Rubio found not only an increasing incidence of violent crime in Latin America during the 1990s but a much higher frequency of violence in crimes against property with levels of 50 per cent in Mexico and Colombia as compared with three per cent in France.[61]

Setting aside these doubts there are clear indications that murder and violent crime are concentrated especially in American cities, north and south, and are especially prevalent in low-income communities. In Colombia, for example, 40 per cent of homicides are highly concentrated in specific areas of ten major cities. In Brazil, where the national rate is not especially high, the rate in São Paolo, a city with a population double that of El Salvador, was about half that of the Central American state, while in the troubled area of Diadema it far exceeded it.[62] Washington, with a rate of 69 per 100,000, was reported by the BBC in 2006 as top of the world's 'murder capitals'. The US capital, the BBC proclaimed, was 170 times more dangerous than the notoriously dull European capital, Brussels, and only three European cities – Moscow, Helsinki and Lisbon – could come anywhere near the nine United States cities included in the poll.[63]

The violence of American cities is not something that has emerged within the last thirty or forty years, though in many instances is has been aggravated by increases in drug trafficking during that period. This, and sporadic rural violence, have been characteristic of the continent for much if its history. The *violencia* in Colombia between 1948 and 1959 in which an estimated 200,000 died throughout the country, the banditry of the Brazilian Sertão, four decades of low level yet ineradicable guerrilla activity in rural Colombia and the prolonged periods of post-war violence that have characterized Central America in recent years and that plagued the United States in the 1860s and 70s are only a few examples of

---

[61] Chaowarit Chaowsangrat, 'Comparative Trends in Violent Crime: the Latin American Context,' citing Mauricio Rubio, 'Los costos de la violencia en América Latina: una crítica al enfoque económica en boga' (San Salvador, 1998), p. 9, accessed at http://www.cerac.org.co/pdf/Comparative Trends in Violent Crime.pdf.

[62] Chaowsangrat, 'Comparative Trends in Violent Crime'.

a kind of violence widespread in the Americas but known only in very small areas on the fringes of Western Europe.

Of the USA, T. J. Stiles writes that:

> It took ten years of peace to reveal the true scale of the Civil War
> ...The massive clash of armies had created the misleading impression
> that this was a conventional war between two sovereign govern-
> ments. The immensity of it masked the smallness of the scale on
> which the war was truly fought. Only the political struggles that
> came after revealed how intimate a conflict it had been all along.[64]

In part this is a matter of settlement. Western Europe, long-settled, was by and large subject to thorough administration by the eighteenth century. This led to the adoption, in spite of Leibniz's critique of the absolutist view peddled by Hobbes, of an ideal of the state as something that saturated the whole of the territory to which it laid claim, providing security and pushing more or less consistent applications of law, confession, taxation and military service through to the finest capillaries and remotest extremities of society.[65]

By contrast, the Americas were unsettled (and unsettling). Think of the way in which American space figured in the eighteenth-century European imagination, by turns utopian and dystopian, but never entirely settled. In a hugely popular and subversive 1731 proto-Romantic novel that went on to inspire operas by Massenet, Puccini and Hans Werner Henze, Antoine François Prévost wrote of the transgression of social barriers by two lovers: the Chevalier Des Grieux and his low-born mistress, the eponymous Manon Lescaut. Fleeing France, they find happiness for a time in New Orleans, where class barriers are less strict. Yet even in Louisiana, political power in the form of the French governor, corrupted by his sexual desire for Manon, drives the lovers into the wilderness that is Louisiana, where Manon dies, leaving a grieving Des Grieux to return to France and take holy orders. Less than two decades later, in 1759, Voltaire notoriously chose South America as the site of all that was best and worst in the world, through which his anti-hero, Candide, pursues his idealized Cunegonde.

---

[63] http://news.bbc.co.uk/2/hi/153988.stm accessed 06/12/2006.

[64] T. J. Stiles, *Jesse James: Last Rebel of the Civil War* (London, 2003), pp. 275–6. The historiographic revision offered by Stiles is echoed in popular culture by the shift from battlefield treatment of the Civil War such as *The Red Badge of Courage* (1951) or *Gettysburg* (1993) to *Cold Mountain* (2003). Many westerns had treated the aftermath of the Civil War, but strictly within their genre.

[65] Gottfried Wilhelm Leibniz, 'Caesarinus Fürstenerius (De Suprematu Principum Germaniae)' [1677] in Patrick Riley (ed.), *Leibniz: Political Writings* (Cambridge, 1972), pp. 111–20.

Returning, finally, to France, he determines to cultivate his garden. America was no garden. Yet in a sense it was. It seems to function in the imagination both as an opportunity to leave a corrupt Old World and re-enter the lost Garden of Eden, and as a new casting out of humanity from the civility of Europe into a less polite world.

Out of this comes a specifically American mental fight, common to the whole of the continent and defined by the antitheses of civilization and barbarism, cultivation and wilderness, plenty and scarcity, law and violence. For violence in representations of the Americas seems always to be paired with the project of imposing order upon it. So while the ideology driving the great experiment of European colonization of the Americas has varied greatly over time and space – at some times and in some places highly individualistic, in others corporatist; here Protestant, there Catholic – one almost omnipresent feature has been the curious conjunction of an almost pedantic respect for law and constitutionality on the one hand and endemic personal and public violence on the other. The origins of gun culture in the United States and its relationship to violent crime remain extremely controversial, as the Bellesiles episode showed, yet surely on any interpretation bespeak a very different relationship between citizen and state to that which has prevailed since the eighteenth century in Western Europe.[66] Whatever the precise connection between the domestic and the social or public, both species of violence have been widespread in this most powerful of the American republics.

Paul A. Gilje, who has extensively studied episodes of public violence in the USA, notes their variety and frequency. In excess of 4,000 riots from the colonial period up to 1970 including riots accompanying lynchings, prison riots, ghetto riots, labour riots and students protests, when taken together seemed to him evidence of the fragility of US democracy and an argument for democratic deepening to avert an even more violent future.[67]

Public violence looms large in the memory. Even Labor Day, the public holiday that celebrates manual workers in the United States, is tainted by violence.

---

[66] Michael A. Bellesiles, *Arming America: the Origins of a National Gun Culture* (New York, 2000) argued that far from being entrenched among sturdy and self-reliant frontiersmen widespread gun ownership was a product of industrialised production of weapons from the 1840s, federal government encouragement, and the Civil War. However the book, highly political because of its implications for the National Rifle Association, was found to be based on defective scholarship and subjected to savage attack. An investigating committee found Bellesiles 'guilty of substandard research methodology and of wilfully misrepresenting specific evidence' (Emory Wheel, 25 October 2002) and he resigned his post (http://www.emorywheel.com/vnews/display.v/ART/2002/10/25/3db9bc0a08df2). Yet he has had his defenders. Was the whole of the book wrong? Can mass production and the Civil War have had no impact?

[67] Paul A. Gilje, *Rioting in America* (Bloomington and Indianapolis, 1996), p. 181.

Just days after signing the bill that effectively made this a national holiday, in 1894, President Grover Cleveland sent in troops to break the Chicago Pullman strike. Often, in the troubled century that followed the Civil War, labour activism, crime and anarchist terrorism (later Communism) became hopelessly confused with one another in the official and public minds. Sometimes the state took deterrent action, as with the 1887 public executions of those held responsible for the deaths of policemen in the Chicago Haymarket Riots or the hugely publicised trials and 1927 executions of Sacco and Vanzetti. On other occasions the state tolerated violence perpetrated against labour by unofficial forces organized by the employers: what would be termed paramilitaries today. As recently as Labor Day 2006, Clancy Sigal reminisced about how he went to Chattanooga, Tennessee with his union-worker mother, Jennie Persily, in the 1930s, where 'the textile factory owners were like feudal barons, with their own armies and the National Guard to break strikes [and] Union organizers could disappear (get killed)'. Persily and Segal were arrested and run out of town.[68] Similar actions, by state and employers, could be cited for most Latin American countries.

To step back from contemporary homicide rates, then, is to encounter high levels of public violence that have long distinguished the Western hemisphere and have often arisen from moral panics in which political and criminal activities have been conflated, in rather the same way that drug trafficking, insurgency and terrorism have fused in contemporary United States perceptions of Colombia. One further element in this muddle surrounding social violence has been race. An abiding theme during the Latin American wars of independence was the elite fear that the struggle for political control might unleash forces of social revolution as had happened in Saint-Domingue.[69] Simón Bolívar, in the course of his long campaign against the Spanish, feared above all '*pardocracy . . . and the extermination of the privileged classes.*' 'He who serves the revolution' – he famously declared in one of his many gloomy moments – 'ploughs the sea.' He continued: 'This country will infallibly fall into the hands of uncontrollable multitudes, thereafter to pass [to] tyrants of all colours and races.'[70] The particular reason for Bolívar's sensitivity on this point was the indispensable military alliance he had formed with the *llaneros*, horsemen from the high plains or *llanos*, a cattle-herding caste of mixed race who, much like the gauchos of the South, formed ferocious and highly effective irregular mounted forces. When the *llanero* leader, General Manuel Piar, began to advocate a war of extermination against

---

[68] *The Philadelphia Inquirer*, 3 September 2006, section B, A11.

[69] C. L. R. James, *The Black Jacobins: Toussaint L'Ouverture and the San Domingo Revolution* (London, 1938); Laurent Dubois, *Avengers of the New World* (Cambridge MA, 2004).

[70] Quotations from Brading, *The First America*, pp. 617 and 618.

all whites, Bolívar had no option but to order his death, and the Liberator remained 'acutely aware of his position as . . . a white man attempting to dominate a population which was largely coloured'.[71]

Frontier extension in advance of central administration in combination with intermittent wars created space in sparsely populated plains and backlands (*sertãos*) throughout the continent in which semi-militarised mongrel populations could not only survive for a time but become, in the hour of their death, emblematic of the nation for triumphant yet wistful settled populations.[72] Cowboys, *llaneros*, gauchos and (Brazilian) gaúchos have much in common.[73]

One fascinating feature of these groups is their racial ambivalence. At one point Martins claims that few of those who lived in the Brazilian backlands were black, because blacks (as slaves until 1888) did not have the opportunity to drop out of society in this way. Later he qualifies this: 'They [the detritus of Portuguese and creole population] were joined by runaway blacks, freed blacks, by mulattos who managed to escape captivity due to being part white, although even mulattos were born slaves.' Later still, he notes that the Canudos War (1897) in the state of Bahia was genocidal, because whatever their literal origin, these people had constituted themselves or been constituted as a sub-race because of their distinctive culture. The same ambivalence is evident in his description of a settlement in *Terra dos Indios* (literally, 'land of the Indians') in Viana, in the state of Maranhão, as 'a place that, given its Negro population, may in fact have been a hideout for runaway slaves'.[74]

Often, the racial intention of social violence in the Americas has been anything but ambiguous. In Colombia, the U'wa people have struggled to defend their land since 2000 against the threat of oilfield development. Activists have been murdered by paramilitary groups on the pretext that they were helping Leftist guerrillas, but the suspicion remains that the motivation may have been to scare them into acquiescence.[75] The campaign of the Embera-Katia Indians against the Sinu River hydro-electric dam that has affected the fish stocks on

---

[71]   Brading, *The First America*, p. 617.

[72]   The term *sertão* is Portuguese and refers to the hinterland of a coast, road or river, but with some additional sense of being less than fully known. Anglo-American 'badlands' is too negative, but something more than merely 'plains,' '*pampas*' or '*llanos*' is needed since, together, they are too restrictive, excluding other terrains and forms of subsistence. Thus, José de Souza Martins refers to an early twentieth-century map of São Paulo in which a third of the territory is described as '*sertão desconhecido*' (unknown backlands). José de Souza Martins, 'Life in the Backlands and the Brazilian Popular Imagination,' (Unpublished conference paper, Cambridge 2001).

[73]   On the gaúchos of Rio Grande do Sul and how they differ from gauchos, see Ruben Olivos, *Tradition Matters: Modern Gaúcho Identity in Brazil* (New York NY, 1996).

[74]   De Souza Martins, pp. 4, 6 and 13. Euclides da Cunha, *Rebellion in the Backlands* (London, 1995).

[75]   http://www.rainforest.org accessed 22 January 2007.

which they depend has also led to attacks by para-militaries.[76] In Brazil, on 4 August 2006, the Federal Supreme Court upheld the conviction of four gold miners who murdered sixteen Yanomami Indians in 1993.[77] Examples could easily be multiplied and the inference is that it is still felt, in the backlands of South and Central America, as it was not so very long ago in the North, that indigenous lives weigh less and may be ended with impunity.

In the North, the clearest instance of the racialization of social violence was lynching: the killing by a mob of someone accused but not tried or convicted of a crime. In the United States it served for many decades as one of the primary instruments of social control, reconciling liberalism with a racially divided society by deterring democratic challenges to elite supremacy. The term originated during the War of Independence, and the practice continued after the war as a way of dealing with cattle thieves, swindlers and rapists. However it took on a particularly racist character from the 1880s, especially in the South, where the end of the Reconstruction era left local authorities free to reassert white authority. No one knows how many people were lynched in the USA up to the end of the 1960s, when the practice largely ceased. The official figure for the period from 1882 (when statistics begin) to 1968 is 4,743. Unreported lynchings may have been equally or more numerous. Yet two things are clear. Lynchings were disproportionately committed against Black Americans and levels of public participation were high, making these events far more powerful than the many unauthorized yet private punitive killings known to have taken place on plantations and in other communities beyond the frontiers of organized justice.

The proportion of blacks to whites among recorded victims is roughly 7:3. Assuming that white lynchings were more likely to be reported (there being more prospect of due process), the prominence of black victims among the unknown total may have been closer to 90 per cent. More certain than this is the fact that though the numbers of victims may seem small in relation to population, the levels of participation in these events were high, with many lynchings advertised in local newspapers with printed tickets available in advance and attended by hundreds of men, women and children, their assembly assisted by specially chartered trains. In short, these unofficial public executions had all the trimmings – including torture and mutilation – that had characterized official executions in Europe up to the early nineteenth century.[78] Assume, in the roundest of figures, an average of a hundred novices at each of 10,000 lynchings between 1882 and 1968 and you will find a million witnesses to violent public

---

[76] http://www.cbc.ca accessed 22 January 2007.

[77] http://www.survival-international.org accessed 22 January 2007.

[78] Although an Act banning public executions in England and Wales did not come into force until 1869, mutilation had been abandoned in the early years of the nineteenth century.

death, perhaps as many as a third of them still alive in the USA today.[79] Beyond them stand the uncounted millions who acquiesced. What properly justifies the designation of lynching as terrorism proper is its use of spectacle and modern technologies of transport and communication to amplify violence.

Callaghan has suggested that one of the consequences of this culture of white violence was to speed black migration to the northern cities and encourage the development of ghettoes there, almost as protective stockades. Another, more insidious consequence may have been to instil a reactive violence in black culture itself of which the plot of John Edgar Wideman's 1973 novel, *The Lynchers*, in which four black men plot to lynch a white policeman, would be nicely emblematic. How else is one to account for the extraordinary levels of unlawful killing in contemporary United States cities and the hugely disproportionate presence of young Blacks among an unusually high prison population?[80]

Working back from high levels of religiosity, the racialization of indigenous Americans and African-Americans and the prevalence of homicide throughout the Americas has revealed differences as well as similarities. There is at least a suggestion that religiosity may correlate positively with income inequality. It is not that the poor seek consolation in religion, but that, in unequal societies, poor and rich alike rely on their faith for different reasons. There is also clear evidence that racism and the systematic disciplining of racialized groups persists in many parts of the Americas. This is evident in the violence routinely directed against rural indigenous populations and inner-city black populations in Brazil where, as in the United States, the prison system strains to cope with a disproportionately black population which, at 371,482, was double the planned capacity in June 2006.[81] It is evident, too, in the impunity of those responsible for the many tens of thousands of deaths – mainly of indigenous people at the hands of government forces – that took place in Guatemala between 1960 and 1996. United States police forces and publics no longer kill with impunity, but the extraordinary levels of incarceration of Black and Latino youth and the persistence of the shameful reservation system (almost a second prison system) suggest a country able to deal with its racial anxieties only through a combination of sublimation and incarceration – church and prison – that sidelines a significant slice of national income into largely unproductive activity.

---

[79]   Robert L. Zangrando, 'Lynching,' in Eric Foner and John A. Garraty (eds.), *The Reader's Companion to American History* (Boston, 1991). See also John F. Callahan in *Oxford Companion to African American Literature* (New York and Oxford, 1997).

[80]   In 2006, close to two-third of the US adult prison population (1,239,946 out of 1,976,019) were Black or Latino, these two groups accounting for only 25 per cent of the total population. In 12 states more than ten per cent of all adult black males were incarcerated (http://www.hrw.org accessed 17 January 2007).

[81]   Human Rights Watch (http://www.hrw.org accessed 17 January 2007).

CHAPTER III

A Grand Scheme and Design

Creating a New World

I have so far followed, informally, a method of contemporary history by which 'it is a definition of the present, and of it alone, that allows us to construct the past and to distinguish in it cleavages or lines of force that lead to the present.'[82] But this analytical method, working backwards from characteristics shared by American republics today to their antecedents, will not deliver up a plot. For this, we must turn to the method of modern history and (not quite the same thing) the history of modernity in the Americas. The method of modern, as distinct from contemporary history is to work forward through time examining the consequences of past events. For the Americas, this might seem to require a starting date of 1492, the arrival of Cristóbal Colon in the New World, or else an even earlier one near the beginning of the fifteenth century, calculated to capture the rise of the great empires that the Europeans were to encounter in Meso-America and the Altiplano. Yet though the creation of a new world in the Americas required the initial destruction of indigenous political communities and the progressive consolidation of creole primacy, it was only when this was followed by a break with imperial parent states inspired by a distinctive vision of society and its possibilities that an American modernity can really be said to have emerged. A date in the later eighteenth century, close to the start of the American wars of independence, begins to make more sense and to sit more comfortably alongside current European and Asian debates about modernity, in which the French Enlightenment, the Industrial Revolution and the extension of formal European administration in Asia and Africa loom large.

---

[82] Jean Baechler, *The Origins of Capitalism* (Oxford, 1975), p. 11.

This shift in the historiography of modernity itself has a history. Once upon a time the schools taught that modern history began when Constantinople fell to the Ottoman Turks in 1453. This marked the final fall of the Roman Empire and, with it, the end of the classical world. The Western Roman Empire had struggled on for a time after the fall of Rome in 410 but came to an end with the deposition of Augustulus by Odovacar, the first Germanic ruler of Italy, in 476. The twilight era separating these events from the fall of the Eastern Empire almost a thousand years later was referred to as mediaeval: literally, between two eras.

What came next was something wholly new and unexpected. The Italian Renaissance, with its enthusiasm for classical forms of decoration and the recovery of classical texts, made it possible to draw contrasts in an unprecedented way between original and copy, classical and modern, at the precise moment when continuity with the classical world evaporated. The modern became conceivable by contrast with the ancient in a Mediterrean space – in Italy above all – where the material debris and entrenched customs of the past were still present. Soon after, the last remaining institution of the ancient world in the West, the Roman Catholic Church, came under attack for its corruption and its claim to an exclusive power of mediation between humankind and God.

The European encounter with an unsuspected and unsuspecting continent at just this point in history, barely forty years after the fall of Constantinople, provided, one might say, the perfect site: the *tabula rasa* on which modernity could be inscribed. Edmundo O'Gorman, in a brilliant series of works from the 1940s through to the early 1960s, showed how the European mind struggled to make sense of this encounter and place it within the traditional chronology of modernity.

There was, after all, no ready-made idea of America. It was not like finding an apple; more like finding something unfamiliar that needed careful handling and just *might* turn out to be a fruit. Spatially, a fourth continent upset late-medieval analogical reasoning in which the three continents of Europe, Asia and Africa mirrored the Trinity and had together formed a perfect (that is to say complete) world enclosed by the ocean. Now instead, a world of four continents embraced the oceans or – still more audaciously – a world had come into being of which the ocean was as much a part as the landmasses.

Either way, the fourth continent set the difficult question of whether the actualization of its potential through history should be by means of imitation or a more autonomous process. Here, for O'Gorman, was the decisive difference between Latin and Anglophone America. The first was mimetic, the second original. 'It was the Spanish part of the invention of America that liberated man from the fetters of a prison-like conception of his physical world,' O'Gorman concluded, 'and it was the English part that liberated him from subordination to

a Europe-centered conception of his historical world. In these two great libera-
tions lies the hidden and true significance of American history.'[83] Deeply sensitive to cultural and religious differences between Anglophone and Spanish-
speaking America, O'Gorman nevertheless found unity in the meaning of
American history at the most abstract level in the concept of liberation.

More mundanely, there was very often, in those who emigrated to the
Americas and the projects they undertook, just such an awareness of emancipation and of possible futures not achievable at home, and this gave rise to a conscious effort to start again and to renounce the Old World, its values and its
customs. An analogy from the industrial world suggests itself. It is often the late
developer that is able to adopt new technology without contributing fully to its
development cost, while older economies remain wedded to outmoded methods, daunted by the magnitude of their sunk costs. So while the project of
modernity might be an aspiration in Europe, inhibited by customary rights and
entrenched institutions, it appeared more realistically achievable in the Americas.
Just as modern Europe came, rightly or wrongly, to regard the Orient as the
antithesis of modernity, it should be no surprise that Domingo Faustino
Sarmiento, one of the leading modernizers in nineteenth-century Argentina,
found that Europe itself provided that foil for America. 'Algiers,' he wrote dis-
missively, 'is enough to give us an idea of the manners and customs of being of
Orientals; because with respect to the Orient, which has so many charms for the
European, its antiquities and traditions are a dead letter for the American. Our
Orient is Europe.'[84]

A Second Modernity

The association of modernity with a sequence of events felt most profoundly in
Western Europe – the Renaissance, the Reformation, the American conquests
– has gradually come to seem parochial to those concerned with world history,
just as it did to Sarmiento a hundred and fifty years ago. There are still indigenous peoples, even in the Americas, whose cosmic calendars do not regard the
arrival of the white people as central.[85] It has therefore become routine in recent

---

[83]   O'Gorman, *Invention of America*, p. 145.

[84]   Domingo Faustino Sarmiento, *Viajes* II, pp. 120 & passim. Quoted in and translated by Ricardo
Cicerchia, 'Journey to the Centre of the Earth,' *Journal of Latin American Studies*, vol. 36, no. 4
(November, 2004), p. 676.

[85]   Olivia Harris, ' "The Coming of the White People": reflections on the Mythologisation of
History in Latin America,' *Bulletin of Latin American Research*, vol. 14, no. 1 (1995), p. 9.

decades to think of modernity as a process originating in the later eighteenth and
early nineteenth centuries and to speak not of one but of multiple modernities.
In part, this has arisen from anti-colonialist reaction. Christopher Bayly, in his
monumental global history, *The Birth of the Modern World*, places himself very
much in this new tradition. He is quite sure that a simple notion of modernity
as diffusion from a core area is mistaken and aligns himself instead with those
'who have insisted on the multicentric nature of globalization in the early modern world'.[86] This is partly because technological advances in what would soon
emerge as the most industrially advanced regions of the world were in part stim-
ulated by effective competition from other parts of the world. Bayly's favourite
example is the stimulus provided to mechanization of the Lancashire cotton
industry from the mid-eighteenth century by cheap high-quality Indian production. 'Technological change,' he insists, 'was multi-centred and global from the
beginning.'[87] By the same token, so was modernity.

Yet though he is concerned to stress the variety and relative autonomy of the
trajectories by which the world has reached its current condition, Bayly has
oddly little to say about the Americas, and never addresses their claim to a privileged position in the history of modernity. This is largely because he has virtually no interest in Latin America while regarding the USA as part of a 'West' that
has too long been seen uncritically as the authentic fount of modernity. My con-
tention, by contrast, is that one might equally well regard the Americas as non-
European, and number them among the multiple and dispersed centres of
modernity, distinguished by the project of creating creole or settler republics
with the aid of coerced labour on the ashes of an indigenous population stunned
and disarmed by Old World diseases.[88]

Clearing the Decks

The European conquest and settlement of the Americas was a long-drawn-
out as well as a bloody affair. Just as the initial Spanish conquests relied upon
exploitation of rivalries within the Meso-American and Andean political systems
rather than military supremacy, so the defeat of residual resistance based in pre-
Columbian sources of legitimacy was hugely assisted by the devastating impact

---

[86]   Bayly, *Modern World*, p. 470.

[87]   Bayly, *Modern World*, p. 174 (citing work by Prasannan Parthasarathi) and again at p. 471.

[88]   The judgment of Felipe Fernandez-Arnesto on the United States might as easily be applied more
generally: '. . . a state founded on usurpation, nurtured through conflict, and expanded at its victims'
expense. . .' That Atlanta policeman really must have felt he had right on his side!

of European diseases. In some regions indigenous population fell by as much as 90 per cent during the century following first contact with Europeans.[89] Newly introduced diseases did most of the work, but brutal suppression of such revolts as there were played its part from the outset, always exacerbated by the mundane genocide practised by European settlers.

A second form of resistance was to be found in maroon states: polities established by escaped slaves of African origin, though sometimes comprising indigenous people as well. Some of these were long-lasting and even formed for a time a peripheral element in the North American system of states. The Spanish recognized Esmereldas, in what is now Colombia, by a treaty of 1599; the British conceded a treaty to a Jamaican maroon state in 1663; Palmares, up country from Pernambuco, endured for most of the seventeenth century in spite of Dutch and Portuguese attempts at suppression.[90] Canudos may be seen as a late example of this phenomenon. One might even include Haiti in this category. Yet with this possible exception all of these were small affairs, with populations numbering no more than a few thousands.[91]

Most formidable, because unmarked by defeat or slavery, were those American polities which remained unconquered. In Araucania, to the South of the captaincy-general of Chile, the Mapuche maintained an independent state throughout the colonial period, and it was not until the 1870s that access to superior weaponry and methods of communication tipped the balance in favour of the settler-state, leading to their confinement to a small reservation in 1883.[92] At much the same time, more recent struggles against nomadic nations in Argentina and the United States were coming to a head. What complicates the picture, in the Americas as in sub-Saharan Africa, is that these struggles were less the last stands of recalcitrant aboriginals against established states than clashes between two distinct classes of modern polities-in-the-making. The economic impact and demonstration effects of earlier European conquest and settlement had prompted the emergence of a new and more extensive kind of polity on the American grasslands in the eighteenth century, fortified by wealth accumulated through trade with the settlers and by access to wild horses and cattle.[93] Neither able nor disposed to challenge Europeans and creoles head-on, leaders of the

---

[89] Brian Hamnett, *A Concise History of Mexico* (Cambridge, 1999), p. 6.

[90] Fernández-Arnesto, *The Americas*, pp. 50–1.

[91] Robert Nelson Anderson, 'The *Quilimbo* of Palmares: a New Overview of a Maroon State in Seventeenth-Century Brazil,' *Journal of Latin American Studies*, vol. 28, no. 3 (October, 1996), pp. 545–566.

[92] Fernández-Arnesto, *The Americas*, p. 68.

[93] Fernández-Arnesto, *The Americas*, p. 123.

Pampas Indians were nevertheless able to mount thousands of fighters and raid as far north as Buenos Aires. Like the Araucanians, they would not finally be subdued until the end of the 1870s, when victory for Julio Roca in his desert campaign proved sufficient to assure him of the presidency. Writing of a not dissimilar emergent indigenous polity in the North, Fernández-Arnesto concludes: '[t]he white man did not introduce imperialism to the Great Plains; he arrived as a competitor with a Sioux empire that was already taking shape.'[94]

Leaving Port

Indigenous and maroon states flicker tantalisingly; old socio-political structures endured at the interstices of modern society; plains nomads took the first steps that might have led to the emergence of an American Genghis Khan or Timur; but the story invariably ended bloodily on the plains, in the hills, up the river, even on the purportedly secure reservations, where First Nations received scant protection and enjoyed little autonomy. Creating a new world meant, first of all, erasing or subordinating the indigenous world. Yet it also meant cutting the bonds with the Old World. Indeed, the two processes were interconnected, for European imperial authorities and religious orders had been inclined, albeit imperfectly and inconsistently, to offer protection to native peoples and to constrain the behaviour of colonists toward them. They did this either from considerations of justice or because of the value of indigenous forces as auxiliaries in the frequent inter-imperial wars that took place on American soil.[95]

So independence, whether from England or Spain, promised to exclude European rivalries from the Americas while simultaneously removing remaining restraints on settler treatment of First Nations. Without it the nineteenth-century genocidal wars of the United States and the Argentine Republic against the plains Indians would probably have been inhibited.

This new world was therefore premised on degrading two classes of relations between states: first of all, those between the European imperial powers in so far as they affected the Americas and between American settler states and their

---

[94] Fernández-Arnesto, *The Americas*, p. 124.

[95] Spanish thought was generally more enlightened than Spanish behaviour. See J. A. Fernández-Santamaría, *The State, War and Peace: Spanish Political Thought in the Renaissance, 1516–1559* (Cambridge, 1977); Bernice Hamilton, *Political Thought in Sixteenth-Century Spain* (Oxford, 1963); Juan Friede and Benjamin Keen (eds.), *Bartolomé de las Casas: toward an understanding of the man and his work* (DeKalb IL, 1971). Fred Anderson's work is full of insight into the intricate relations between imperial, colonial, and indigenous forces: *Crucible of War: the Seven Years' War and the Fate of Empire in British North America, 1754–1766* (London, 2001). So too is James Fennimore Cooper, *The Last of the Mohicans*.

erstwhile masters, which came to be regarded as corrupt, exploitative, imperti-
nent and bellicose; secondly, those with indigenous peoples, whose status as
political communities and continuity with a pre-Columbian order was whenever
possible denied or traduced. And if this process of suppression was never finally
to be completed, it had still been clear from the start that – temporary accommodations aside – there was to be no question of a mixed society of native and
settler states in the Americas. This much had already been made manifest in the
South by Viceroy Toledo's execution of Tupac Amaru, the last Inca, in 1573,
and it began to emerge in the North with the gradual adoption of extirpative or
unlimited warfare in Virginia and New England during the first half of the seventeenth century.[96] While the protection granted to indigenous peoples by the
Crowns of Spain and England and their usefulness as guides and auxiliaries in the
frequent wars between European powers might delay things for a time, final and
total subjugation was now only a matter of time.

The Archipelago of Modernities

Building a new world required destruction and a Nietzschean forgetfulness of the
past. It was also a project grounded in a revolutionary view of the future and distinctive notions of modernity. Hannah Arendt argued that the very idea of revolution was American in origin. 'Symbolically speaking' – she continued – 'one
may say that the stage was set for revolutions in the modern sense of a complete
change of society, when John Adams, more than a decade before the actual outbreak of the American Revolution, could state: "I always consider the settlement
of America as the opening of a grand scheme and design in Providence for the
illumination of the ignorant and the emancipation of the slavish part of mankind
all over the earth".'[97] But if true revolution originated in the Americas then so,
too, did its lusty sibling, modernity. Later, Gertrude Stein would rail against
those who called the United States a new country. It was the oldest of countries,
she protested, because it had, by the manner of its civil war, been the first to
enter modernity.[98] 'America' – Baudrillard assures us – 'is the original version of
modernity', before going entirely off the rails, railing as only Baudrillard could.[99]

---

[96]   Henry Kamen, *Spain's Road to Empire: The Making of a World Power, 1492–1763* (London, 2002),
pp. 193–5; Grenier, *The First Way of War*, pp. 21–9.

[97]   Hannah Arendt, *On Revolution* [1963] (London, 1973), p. 23.

[98]   Gertrude Stein, *The Autobiography of Alice B. Toklas* [1933] (Harmondsworth, 1966), p. 103.
A case can be made for the Crimean war, a decade before, with its use of narrow gauge railway and
industrialised treatment of casualties, but morphine and barbed wire probably clinch it for the US.

[99]   Jean Baudrillard, *America* (London and New York, 1988), p. 76.

What little Bayly does have to say about the Americas is often oddly out of focus. Brazil, we are told, was 'the great success story' in Latin America after 1840 because coffee exports allowed it to finance its external debt more effectively than its Hispanic neighbours and achieve earlier political stability. This is challengeable in almost every particular. In terms of per capita income Argentina easily exceeded Brazil up to the mid-twentieth century. Political stability owed less to economic conditions than to the decision of the Braganzas to move their court to Brazil when the peninsula was overrun by Napoleon in 1807. Legitimacy was preserved thanks to a handy British warship. Easier borrowing had less to do with export income than the decision to allow Rothschilds a monopoly instead of following the Argentine example and playing the field.

At other times it is the silence that is striking. Noting the hardening of racial barriers in the USA in the later nineteenth century, manifest in the substitution of segregation for slavery, the exclusion of Asian immigrants, and mounting pressure on First Nations, Bayly's impulse is to compare this with parallel developments in Britain's colonies of settlement in North America, Australasia and South Africa.[100] The so-called 'White Dominions' within the British empire were, it is perfectly true, 'American' in many respects, but never as American as the Spanish-American republics.

The obvious comparator here is surely Argentina, where the wars of annihilation against indigenous peoples were most closely comparable with US experience. But, resisting the obvious, consider Ecuador. This small South American country, like the giant to its north, experienced a civil war, ending in 1895, in which a Liberal victory shifted power from the traditional landowning elite to a coastal commercial bourgeoisie committed to the development of a secular state, a more flexible labour market and closer integration with world markets. Yet, as Nicola Foote put it, in words that might almost have been written of the USA, 'ideas of universality and inclusion were mediated by the reality of the existence of large populations of racially subordinate groups, who had been excluded by previous regimes.'[101] So although black and indigenous troops had contributed largely to the Liberal victory, they were to be disappointed by the peace. The creole state denied them their due share in the fruits of victory, wrote them out of the official histories of the war and stigmatized them as violent, sexually impulsive and idle. Newly arriving migrants from the West Indies and China prompted moral panics, while the government vainly sought to whiten the population by the offer of free passage, land and municipal autonomy to West Europeans.

---

[100] Bayly, *Modern World*, pp. 226–7.

[101] Nicola Foote, 'Race, State and Nation in early Twentieth-Century Ecuador,' *Nations and Nationalism* vol. 12, no. 2 (April 2006), p. 262.

Yet far from exploring, let alone embracing, American commonalities, Bayly strains every nerve to drive a wedge between North and South, performing considerable gymnastics to exaggerate the rise of the modern state in the USA and deny it in Latin America.[102] In a denial of that anarchism which has been one of the most attractive features of the USA, he identifies civil society organizations as harbingers of the modern state rather than means to avert it and goes on to draw a contrast with Latin America where 'political leaders attempted to emulate the continental European model' while 'military-dominated regimes emerged after independence' and 'in the hinterland, the politics of the Creole magnates and Amerindian village leaders constantly impeded the development of centralised power'. Forget that Argentina consolidated a republic that would endure with little constitutional irregularity for seven decades at the very moment when the United States split bloodily asunder! Forget that Washington has still not quite managed to stamp out polygamy in Utah and neighbouring states![103] Forget that Uruguay was among the pioneers of twentieth-century welfare capitalism![104]

More recently, Laurence Whitehead has provided a far more nuanced and complex synthetic view of Latin American modernity, which he regards as distinctive in several ways. Once again, however, the analysis is vitiated by too easy an assumption of the unity of a West that conjoins Europe and Anglophone America. Latin America was marked off from the rest of the non-West from the outset, Whitehead argues, by the total implausibility of any return to pre-conquest authenticity. But it was also marked off from the West by 'the uneven and incomplete manner in which successive projects and models … have been assimilated'.[105]

This, as Whitehead is quick to point out, is not an argument that lends itself to quantification. It may be that the more complex political structures of advanced industrial countries cushioned the impact of successive modernist projects, knocking the rough edges off them. It may be that in Latin America the less constrained power of modernizing elites led to ill-judged imposition of unrealistic plans, prompting hostile popular reactions. Yet it is hard not to feel that modernity has always and everywhere been fragmented, contested, imposed and incomplete. So to some minds Whitehead's striking image of a landscape littered with the wrecks

---

[102] Bayly, *Modern World*, p. 258.

[103] BBC (http://news.bbc.co.uk/1/hi/world/America/1329977.stm, accessed 22 January 2007).

[104] Simon G. Hanson, *Utopia in Uruguay: Chapters in the Economic History of Uruguay* (New York, 1938).

[105] Laurence Whitehead, *Latin America: A New Interpretation* (New York and Houndmills, 2006), p. 35.

of modernism will call forth as many European and North American images as Latin American. The Panama Canal is indeed 'a monument that has now become a relic'. But so is the Manchester Ship Canal. So was the Birmingham inner ring road until inspired urban planning and heavy investment relieved the stranglehold it had on Britain's second city during the 1990s. If Havana is an exhibit in the mausoleum of modernity, then why not Baltimore?[106] If the Welsh speakers of Patagonia or the Mennonite settlers in Bolivia, why not the Amish in Pennsylvania or the Mormons of Salt Lake City? Whitehead anticipates the challenge. He concedes that Latin America may not be distinctive. Yet none of the counter-examples he then goes on to consider are from the USA or Western Europe.[107] There is too easy an assumption of a well-formed modernity accomplished in the Western core.

One answer to Whitehead's image of Latin America as a mausoleum of modernities is surely that all the achievements of modernity are doomed, because the process of modernization is one of constant supersession. But the landscape is dominated by the mausoleum only when there is insufficient capital for the living evidences of modernity to obscure the dead and when the style of modernity is not even partly autochthonous.

If the first of these conditions is not met, modernity can be judged to have failed, like a leaven that stops fermenting. Renewing the leaven need not be a matter of high technology. Even the ruins of past modernities can make money. Reminding his readers that the Fray Bentos meat processing plant in Uruguay was 'perhaps briefly the largest slaughterhouse in the world', David Edgerton goes on to tell us how to visit the plant, now a museum.[108] It is another case entirely with Cuban sugar, rightly placed by Alan Dye alongside meat-packing, steel and chemicals at the cutting edge of the second industrial revolution.[109] It is simply hanging on.

If the second condition of living modernity – some measure of autochthonous invention – is not met, then the country is subsumed within a globalized culture, and since this bears such strong marks of the United States, we may as well say that – for Latin America – this amounts to becoming doubly American or else no longer authentically American: it hardly matters which. Few know that

---

[106] Baltimore has its charms, not least the Matisses in the Cone Collection, and is selected because of its early slipping away from the front-line of modernity, displaced by New York. See Robert Greenhalgh Albion, *The Rise of New York Port, 1815–1860* (New York and London, 1939).

[107] Whitehead, *Latin America*, pp. 49–51.

[108] David Edgerton, 'Slower Technology,' *Prospect*, 13[1] (February, 2007). To visit, see http://www.anglo.8m.com or contact Rene Boretto on rboretto@adinet.com.uy.

[109] Richard Dye, *Cuban Sugar in the Age of Mass Production: Technology and the Economics of the Sugar Central, 1899–1929* (Stanford CA, 1998).

the self-propelled combine-harvester, marketed from the late 1930s by the Canadian Massey-Harris Company, was conceived, and its eight prototypes tested in Argentina, after a determined campaign by Australian and Argentine managers in the company's Buenos Aires branch.[110] Sensitive to the vulnerability of their sugar exports to mounting protectionism in the USA, engineers at the US-owned Grace Company in Peru turned their attention to making paper out of sugar-cane waste. From this came a paper-chemicals complex that would develop plastics by the 1960s.[111]

Peru indeed presents a fascinating study in modernity outside the United States (though Argentina, Cuba, Colombia or Canada would serve equally well). Jennifer Fraser has suggested that it was in reaction to the humiliation of defeat and occupation during the War of the Pacific that Peru so enthusiastically adopted science as a route to modernity and redemption.[112] Anticipating this intuition, Paul Gootenberg traced the history of a modern pharmaceutical industry in Peru, based on coca leaves, to its end in the later 1940s, defeated by US-led criminalization of cocaine.[113] In such ways Peru reached the further shores of post-modernity after only the briefest of crossings. It was no mere coincidence that the postmodernism of Vargas Llosa should emerge in Peru. It had already been fed by the ironies of appropriated and frustrated modernities that had contributed to the remarkable poetic insights of César Vallejo (1892–1938). Anticipating Kurt Vonnegut's astonishing response to modern warfare, surely the most profound (and American) war novel of the twentieth century, Vallejo suggested that modernity was about living simultaneously in several times: medieval, baroque, contemporary.[114]

Was all this Peruvian or American? I intend only to claim that Latin America was, and sometimes is modern, while conceding that, one way or another, the reach of US manufacturing multinationals was over-riding older geographies and setting the economic terms of engagement by the middle of the twentieth

---

[110] E. P. Neufeld, *A Global Corporation: A History of the International Development of Massey-Ferguson Limited* (Toronto, 1969), p. 36 and 338.

[111] Lester D. Langley, *The Americas in the Modern Age* (New Haven and London, 2003), p. 123, citing Laurence A. Clayton, *Peru and the United States: the Condor and the Eagle* (Athens GA, 1999), pp. 142–49.

[112] Jennifer Fraser, Birkbeck College, University of London. Unpublished paper at the annual conference of the Society of Latin American Studies, University of Derby, 2005.

[113] Paul Gootenberg, 'Reluctance or Resistance? – Constructing Cocaine (Prohibitions) in Peru, 1910–1950,' in Paul Gootenberg (ed.), *Cocaine: Global Histories* (London, 1999), pp. 46–79.

[114] William Rowe, Birkbeck College, University of London. Unpublished paper at the annual conference of the Society of Latin American Studies, University of Derby, 2005; Kurt Vonnegut, Jr., *Slaughterhouse 5 or The Children's Crusade: A Duty Dance with Death* [1969].

century, so that it makes progressively less sense to think of American modernity in national terms at all.

If, finally, both conditions of a living modernity are met, as in the USA, then the catacombs of past modernities house a bank of superseded models from which sub-cultures and variants of the currently dominant strand of modernity may draw, swaddling continuing technological innovation in modish replication and kitsch.

Much of what is to be said about modernity in the core is true also of the periphery. Many of the points Whitehead makes about the Latin American pre-occupation with modern cartography, the taxonomy of natural resources and the statistical representation of the new Latin American nations are equally true of the United States.[115] So the decisive points are that the USA stops being to any significant extent a copier and becomes an innovator from the 1840s onward, and that its economy, by this time, affords the economies of scale needed for autochthonous development. As we saw in chapter 1, the fortunes of war and the sheer materiality of the continental USA trump cultural essentialism when it comes to explaining US exceptionalism. But though some account has been offered of how fiscal disintegration acted as a brake on Hispanic America, little has yet been said about what was driving the United States. This turns out to be quite simple. The United States, like much of the Americas, lacked *skilled* labour. There was therefore profit to be made from anything that economised on this scarce resource. Mass production methods did just this by breaking down processes that had formerly been the exclusive province of the master craftsman into a series of simple tasks. Adam Smith had foreseen this, and had also foreseen that such division of labour was constrained by the size of the market. What he had perhaps not foreseen was that when mass production was applied to products that in their turn economized on scarce skilled labour, releasing it for other purposes, the gains were compounded. So the Colt Company took the manufacture of firearms from the artisanal workshop into the factory, but it was the Singer Sewing Machine that first produced the compound effect, adding – to mass production of the machine itself – the possibility of mass production of clothing, releasing domestic labour into the marketplace.[116]

When combined with massive increases in agricultural productivity facilitated by artificial fertilizers, the mechanization of farming and food production and the development of modern grain elevators, such products as these – the refrigerator,

---

[115]   See, for example, John Rennie Short, *Representing the Republic: Mapping the United States, 1600–1900* (London, 2001).

[116]   Raymond Vernon, 'International Investment and International Trade in the Product Cycle,' *Quarterly Journal of Economics*, vol. 80, no. 2 (May, 1966).

the motor car, the vacuum cleaner, the washing machine – made possible higher standards of living in the United States by the later nineteenth century than had ever before been attained. Anthony Trollope, journeying through the United States in 1861, could already see both things – the innovations and the wealth – though he did not explicitly link them. 'The great glory of the Americans,' he marvelled, 'is in their wondrous contrivances . . . Soda-water bottles open themselves without any trouble of wire or strings. Men and women go up and down stairs without motive power of their own'.[117] Wealth, too, was already apparent to Trollope, travelling in 1861, who refers repeatedly to per capita meat consumption in the USA as being double that in Britain and several times notes the lack of beggars. 'In any large town in England,' he declares at one point, 'it is probable that a higher excellence of education would be found than in Milwaukee, and also a style of life into which more of refinement and luxury had found its way. But the general level of these things, of material and intellectual well-being – of beef, that is, and book learning – is no doubt infinitely higher in a new American than in an old European town. Such an animal as a beggar is as much unknown as a mastodon. Men out of work or in want are almost unknown.' [118]

Reconciling the Exception

Having elaborated and partly conceded O'Gorman's distinction between a mimetic Latin and an originary Anglo-America, it is well to recall his insistence on liberation as the unifying theme of the Americas, my own emphasis on the liberal aspirations shared by creole elites throughout the hemisphere and the ways in which both these understandings rule off the Americas from Europe. Bayly pays too little attention to America. Whitehead neglects the defining quality of incompleteness that haunts modernity even in the United States and confuses achievement and aspiration in his treatment of Latin America. Latin Americans generally failed, but they were engaged in the same enterprize as their northern cousins. Concede this, accept the dismissal of cultural and institutional arguments for divergence in the Americas offered in earlier chapters, and it may

---

[117] Trollope, *North America*, p. 73. Note, though, his hatred of central heating (pp. 107, 90, 115 and 123). 'As to the hot-air pipes, there can, I think, be no doubt that to them is to be charged the murder of all rosy cheeks throughout the States.' Of the young ladies of Fifth Avenue, New York City, he writes: 'The very pith and marrow of life is baked out of their young bones by the hot-air chambers to which they are accustomed. Hot air is the great destroyer of American beauty.' (p. 115).

[118] Trollope, *North America*, p. 78.

still remain something of a mystery how any original unity of predicament can have withstood the vast natural material disparity that opened up during the nineteenth century, even if that disparity was in large measure the outcome of a mix of good luck, judicious purchases and the timely application of lethal force.

Surely the United States got where it did in the nineteenth and twentieth centuries by adopting more liberal economic policies based in the sanctity of private property, individualism and sheer hard work? Surely this holds even if its root was not Protestantism but the mundane desire of immigrants to better themselves? Surely the processes that would place the United States in a 'First' and Bolivia in a 'Third' world, separated now by an unbridgeable chasm after the collapse of Communism, must have been fundamentally different?

Yet even this fall-back argument for the distinctiveness of the United States collapses under interrogation, leaving economic liberalism as just one more characteristic of its recent deviation from continental norms. Economic policy, for much of the past two hundred years, has not been so very different in the USA as compared with other American states. In this, as in so much else, the USA has been discernibly American. Once again it was the outcomes that diverged, not the projects nor even the methods by which they were characteristically pursued.

America had first to be imagined and then, in an entirely mundane and material fashion, to be built. Though much had been done in the colonial era there remained, in the early nineteenth century, frontiers of settlement throughout the hemisphere and a set of tasks quite distinct from those facing Western Europe, in which creation was more to the fore than transformation of traditional economies.

Once creole states were established, following the wars of independence, the remaining task was quite literally one of construction: the construction of transport systems, settlements, utilities and all the paraphernalia of national economies. Without established sources of revenue it was inevitable that tariffs would be the main source of funds for the states that set about this task. Many were federations. Lacking effective means to extract revenue from the component states, their central authorities were doubly reliant on customs duties collected at the principal ports.

This is all well known. How odd, then, to find Jeffrey Williamson, who has done more than anyone else in recent years to clarify long-run tariff levels the world over, getting into a muddle about tariffs in the Americas. 'Latin American governments' – he and his co-author assure us – 'did not switch from liberal to protectionist policies during the Great Depression or during the decade after. Latin America had already been highly protectionist for more than a century.'[119]

---

[119]   John H. Coatsworth and Jeffrey G Williamson, 'Always Protectionist? Latin American Tariffs from Independence to Great Depression,' *Journal of Latin American Studies*, vol. 36, no. 2 (May, 2004), p. 205.

This passage is doubly surprising. First of all it confuses high tariffs with protectionism. Secondly, it remarks on high tariffs as a peculiar feature of Latin America even though it is clear from other publications by Williamson that high tariffs were a feature of the Americas as a whole, USA included, during the nineteenth and early twentieth centuries, and that they were generally driven by revenue needs rather than any desire to foster infant industries. Regarding the first point, it is evident from a 2003 paper by Williamson that European settler states had the highest tariffs of any group in the nineteenth century: higher than Asia, the core of industrialized states, or the peripheral European group. Moreover, their average rate would have been even higher had the United States been allocated to this group rather than to the industrial core (or the West, as we may call it).[120]

The second oddness concerns the timing of Latin America's move to protectionism. The point of the 2004 paper is to attack the general assumption that Latin American countries were liberal open economies up to the 1930s, and only then veered off on a doomed course of import-substituting industrialization and heavy-handed state intervention, charted by Argentine economist Raúl Prebisch and more remotely influenced by John Maynard Keynes. The motive was to guard against any repetition of the mauling they had received during the 1920s and 1930s as world prices of primary products slumped. By 1933 the wholesale price index for Argentine rural goods had fallen to 57 per cent of its 1926 level, not to recover until wartime demand came to the rescue in the 1940s. [121] But there is much more to protectionism than high tariffs. The 1930s lurch included other measures, such as exchange controls, national management of export marketing, state ownership of strategic industries, the creation of central banks. Moreover, it was part of a tendency from which it is hard to exclude Roosevelt's New Deal in the United States itself.

Besides, if any American countries were pioneers of protectionism in the full sense of the word earlier on, they were surely Canada and the USA. Clearly protectionist tariffs to propitiate the populist rebels of 1837 were imposed on farm products in 1843 and selected manufactured items in 1847. Right through to the 1930s, details of the level and structure of the tariff were matters that commanded Prime Ministerial attention in Canada.[122] In the USA, a mix of interest and anti-imperialist sentiment led to a strong reaction against the dominance of British textile exports in the 1820s. This had not been helped by Henry

---

[120] Jeffrey G. Williamson, 'Was it Stolper-Samuelson, Infant Industry or Something Else? World Tariffs 1789–1938,' NBER Working Paper 9656 (Cambridge MA, 2003).

[121] Harry S. Ferns, *The Argentine Economy, 1516–1971* (Newton Abbot, 1973), p. 129.

[122] D. G. Creighton, 'The Economic Background of the Rebellions of 1837,' *Canadian Journal of Economic and Political Science*, vol. 3, no. 3 (August, 1937), pp. 324–5.

Brougham's 1816 suggestion that British merchants dump goods in the USA to 'stifle in the cradle those rising manufactures . . . which the war had forced into existence contrary to the natural course of things'.[123]

In 1824, in order to encourage local manufacture, the US federal government increased import duties on British woollens. The British government responded with a finely calculated countervailing reduction in its own tariff on imports of raw wool. But this, coupled with a sharp commercial crisis in 1827, aggravated anti–British feelings.[124] Things went from bad to worse as British firms attempted to avoid the full force of the tariff by under-invoicing goods consigned to friendly merchant houses on the eastern seaboard of the USA, a ruse that was met with arrests and lengthy litigation.[125] The Americans responded in 1828 with what became known as the 'tariff of abominations', with 45 per cent *ad valorem* duties on woollens and iron goods. Robert Peel counselled Colonial Secretary William Huskisson against further retaliation, and there the matter rested for the time being.[126] Later, US tariffs rose above the Latin American average in the years following the Civil War while, not long afterwards, a recently federated and self-governing Canada embarked on an explicitly protectionist course with the National Policy of 1878, built around the tariff and intended to foster industrialization, not merely to raise revenue.[127] The higher tariff was presented as nationally integrative because it would encourage a wider range of activities and stimulate inter-provincial trade. Prime Minister Macdonald felt the slight welfare loss to be suffered in the short term a fair price to pay, arguing that there were 'national considerations that rise far higher than mere accumulation of wealth,' and that 'no nation has ever arisen whose policy was Free-Trade'.[128]

This is not the place to embark on lengthy consideration of the tariff history of the Americas. What is clear is that high tariffs were a feature common to all the countries of the New World, that their main purpose up to 1914 was revenue and that the countries that were quickest to move on to deliberately protectionist use of the tariff were the USA and British North America, with Latin

---

[123]   Quoted in Edward P. Crapol, *America for Americans: Economic Nationalism and Anglophobia in the late Nineteenth Century* (Westport CO, 1973), p. 8.

[124]   J. B. Williams, *British Commercial Policy and Trade Expansion, 1750–1850* (Place, 1972), p. 241.

[125]   Herbert Heaton, 'Yorkshire Cloth Traders in the US, 1770–1840,' in G.D. Lumb and W.B. Crump (eds.), *The Thoresby Miscellany*, vol. 11 (Leeds, 1945).

[126]   R.G. Wilson, *Gentleman Merchants: the Merchant Community in Leeds, 1700–1830* (Manchester and New York, 1971), chapter 6.

[127]   V. C. Fowke, 'The National Policy, Old and New,' *Canadian Journal of Economics and Political Science*, vol. 18, no. 3 (August, 1952).

[128]   D. W. Goodwin, *Canadian Economic Thought: The Political Economy of a Developing Nation, 1814–1914* (Durham NC, 1961).

America trailing. It was not in Latin America but in the United States that the modern doctrines of economic nationalism were developed by Alexander Hamilton and the Careys, father and son. Like the theory of capitalist imperialism, also an offspring of the United States invention, they would in due course be turned against a bewildered parent.[129]

A similar story can be told about foreign investment. By the later 1820s many Latin American states had defaulted on loans issued in London in the first flush of post-independence enthusiasm. There were to be further waves of default in the 1970s and the early 1890s. But the United States was no saint, with defaults by individual states in the 1830s, 1850s and 1870s. In spite of these disappointments British liberals persisted, almost to the end of the century, in regarding all of independent America as a land free from aristocracy, in which more rational and constitutional forms of economic development and international relations might be looked for, fixing upon the United States, above all, as the place in which their ideals might be worked out without compromise. In doing so, they established what might be termed the White Legend: a legend of economic liberalism in the Americas.

Richard Cobden, whose pamphlets constantly held up British gains from trade with the independent United States of America as an argument against imperialism and war, was among many British liberals to put his money where his mouth was. Loans to European autocracies such as Austria or Russia, let alone the Turk, were morally unacceptable because they would be invested in unprofitable military equipment. By the same token they were financially unsound.[130] He himself invested heavily in the Illinois Central Railway. A contemporary commented that Cobden 'viewed his investments in an entirely different light from that in which they would be seen by an ordinary man of business. He thought of the overcrowded cities of Europe. His mind surveyed at a glance the vast expanses of rich unoccupied virgin land in the mighty valley of the Mississippi, and he came to the conclusion that the demand for the company's land would be both great and immediate.'[131] It wasn't, and Cobden had some trouble meeting calls on the shares. Thus did ideology cloud contemporary visions of the Americas and, in due course, their history.

Often irresponsible or corrupt in their application of borrowed funds, American states remained by and large welcoming to foreign capital until the 1870s. Thereafter, a reaction set in, especially against direct foreign investment,

---

[129] Norman Etherington, *Theories of Imperialism: War, Conquest and Capital* (London, 1984).

[130] Peter Cain, 'Capitalism, War and Internationalism in the Thought of Richard Cobden,' *British Journal of International Studies*, vol. 5, no. 3 (October, 1979), p. 245.

[131] John Morley, *The Life of Richard Cobden* [1879] (London: 1905), p. 884.

where managerial control was exerted from Europe. The fact that this movement, peaking in the 1890s, was known as populism in the USA and economic nationalism elsewhere cannot obscure the similarities. Here is a further reason why the Coatsworth and Williamson suggestion that Latin America uniquely was 'always protectionist' is misleading. Economic xenophobia would peak in Mexico under Cardenas in the 1930s and Peron's Argentina the following decade. It would peak a second time during the 1970s. But its first flowering came in the 1880s and 1890s with attempts to introduce differential taxation weighted against foreign firms, to force European fire insurance companies and banks to hold reserves in local government bonds, and the like. That the USA escaped the 1930s wave was largely a consequence of the low levels of British investment there following extensive sales of dollar assets during the Great War. Toward the end of the 1970s and in the 1980s there was an element of xenophobic comment in the US press directed at UK and Japanese FDI, at a time when it stood way below typical levels of US FDI in European countries. In short, the US has remained sensitive on this point, restrained only by the extent and vulnerability of its own global corporate interests.

Back in the 1880s they were more than just sensitive. A wave of recent British purchases of ranching, mining, brewing and milling companies in the United States was readily interpreted by small and middling farmers 'either as a step in the formation of great monopolies, or, even worse, as part of an imperialistic design conceived by London bankers to enslave the American people'.[132] Press campaigns stoked the boiler, and William Jennings Bryan directed the resultant steam into partially successful attempts to secure state and federal legislation against foreign land ownership. 'One of the principal attractions to Britons in conducting operations in the trans-Mississippi West had been the stability and respect for property rights characteristic of American society in the past,' one historian concluded, 'but the Bryan program seemed to represent repudiation and despoiliation.'[133]

The story can be replicated in Uruguay, Peru, and any number of Latin American countries. The point is that the USA was little different, and also shared the extraordinary ambivalence of Argentina and Venezuela (if not of others) about natural resources, believing itself to be, from one moment to the next, the most abundant and well supplied of economies (*un país tan rico!*) and the most vulnerable. Moreover, the economic nationalist tendency in United States commercial policy lasted well into the mid-twentieth century. Close and

---

[132]   Roger V. Clements, 'The Farmers' Attitude toward British Direct Investment in American Industry,' *Journal of Economic History*, vol. 15, no. 2 (1955), p. 151.
[133]   Clements, 1955, pp. 227–8.

deeply interested observers of Washington, the British Foreign Office were convinced up to 1943 that the post-war world would see a resumption of the bilateral trading relations and spheres of influence that had characterised the 1930s. The general view in the Board of Trade in 1942 was that 'after the war the United States Government may wish to lay the foundations of hemispheric containment in the strategic sphere, which may, in certain circumstances, extend to self-sufficiency.' A year later, at the Foreign Office, the ideas of Sumner Welles on the post-war position of the United States were being condemned as 'almost indistinguishable from the doctrines of Lebensraum – *el imperialismo yanqui* with a vengeance'.[134] How surprising, then, and even un-American, was the sudden and partial lurch of the United States, over the next year, toward multilateralism and economic liberalism, summed up in Henry Morgenthau's declaration, at the Bretton Woods conference, of an end to economic nationalism. *Pace* Coatsworth and Williamson, the point is not that Latin America did or did not lurch towards neomercantilism in the 1930s and '40s, but that the United States lurched, uncharacteristically and incompletely, toward economic liberalism.

The Primacy of Economics

Because the American project of modernity was as much or more to do with creole control of the territories and subordinate populations of the continent as with the constitution of republics, the relationship between state and market tended to veer, as we have seen, toward policies that would be termed mercantilist or nationalist in the Old World. This primacy of the economic was almost unavoidable in American conditions. Though states might be relatively weak they were also everywhere and indispensable in the process of nation building. European immigrants by the million were wrenched from their communities by the prospect of reward and freedom. This process endorsed the primacy of market over political community. When the United States came to believe in the 1940s that the fundamental cause of the Second World War lay in the way economic failure rather than instrinsically political catastrophe had facilitated the emergence of totalitarianism, it was a further evidence of the primacy of economics in American culture. When Chilean Marxists decided in the 1960s that political transformation required autarky, the same mentality was in play.

The centrality of economic development within the American project meant that American liberalism, in this as in its exclusion of racialized populations, was

---

[134] Charles A. Jones, *El reino unido y América: inversions e influencia económica* (Madrid, 1992) p. 211. See also references to the relevant primary sources in Chapter 4, no. 173 of the present work.

always bound to be less than liberal by European standards. The American state was associated more with nation-building than with inter-state and high intensity war-fighting.[135] Joseph Schumpeter would famously argue that the United States was not and never could be imperialist, since imperialism, which he defined as an objectless disposition to violence on the part of the state, was a product of atavistic hereditary aristocracies, stranded in a newly capitalist European world.[136] In an odd way he was right. While Tsarist Russia supported a large standing army but had to bring in Scots to run its strategic railways, the major railroads in the United States – locally managed though reliant on British portfolio investment – were larger organizations than the federal state or its armed forces up to the early twentieth century.[137] These are ways of saying that in the Americas, following independence, the state was more often hitched to the locomotive of economic development than in Europe, where mercantilist states had too often drawn dependent capitalism in their train.[138] And the residue of this inverted relationship between state and economy was that for twentieth-century Americans, the major landmarks would be economic fluctuations: the Great Depression of the 1930s, the long boom of the 1950s and 60s, the periods of prosperity brought by the World Wars, the debt crisis of the 1980s, the implementation of neo-liberal reforms and so on, while, for Europeans, these would be dwarfed by the dates of major hostilities: 1914–18, 1939–45, 1947–89.

The important exception, once again, is the United States of America, which through interventions in 1917, and after 1941, became a European as well as an American (and indeed an Asian) power. And this is born out in the contrast between routine Anglo-American academic treatment of twentieth-century international relations and Latin American writings on the same subject. The first – regardless of school or methodology – were for many years obsessed with the causes, conduct, and resolution of armed conflicts: 'Peace Studies' no less than 'War Studies'. Only toward the end of the 1970s was an older United States preoccupation with international economic relations revived when International Political Economy emerged as a significant sub-discipline within International

---

[135]   Miguel Centeno, *Blood and Debt: War and the Nation-State in Latin America* (University Park PA, 2002).

[136]   Joseph A. Schumpeter, *Imperialism and Social Classes* [c.1917] (Oxford, 1951).

[137]   Dorothy B. Adler, *British Investment in American Railways, 1934–1898* (Charlottesville, 1970); David Vogel, 'Whay Businessmen Distrust Their State: The Political Consciousness of American Corporate Executives,' *British Journal of Political Science*, vol. 8, no. 1, pp. 58–9.

[138]   On relations between Bismark and his banker, where the former cracked the whip, see Fritz Stern, *Gold and Iron: Bismark, Bleichröder, and the Building of the German Empire* (London, 1977).

Relations.[139] Latin America, by contrast, while sharing the enthusiasm for geopolitics of some of its northern neighbours in its staff colleges, elsewhere showed real originality in its treatment of international economic affairs, producing at least three distinct waves of heterodox analysis: nationalist, structuralist, and *dependentista*.[140]

---

[139] The pioneers were Charles Kindleberger, *Power and Money: the Economics of International Politics and the Politics of International Economics* (London, 1970) and Klaus Knorr, *Power and Wealth: the Political Economy of International Power* (New York, 1973).

[140] Leading examples of the three streams are Francisco A. Encina, *Nuestra Inferioridad Económica* [1911] (Santiago de Chile, 1986); UNCTAD, *Nueva política para el desarrollo. Informe de Raúl Prebisch [sercretario general] a la Conferencia de la Naciones Unidas sobre Comercio y Desarrollo* . . . (Mexico City, 1964), and Andre Gunder Frank, *Latin America: underdevelopment or revolution. Essays on the development of underdevelopment and the immediate enemy* (New York, 1969).

CHAPTER IV

American International Society

Diplomacy, international law, international organization, the balance of power, great power management and warfare are the means by which states relate to one another. To the extent that these institutions presuppose, generate and reproduce norms of state behaviour, relations between states form an international society.[141] This understanding has recently been applied to Latin America with skill and scholarship by Arie Kacowicz.[142] Can it; ought it to be taken a step further, to include the United States? To do so is to encounter a blend of norms specific to the hemisphere and very different from those in Europe or in global relations between major powers. There has been more emphasis on law and organization, more intrusive and coercive great power management, less war and virtually no balancing. It is this distinctive form of international society that provides the theme of this chapter.

It should be no surprise to find the peculiarly American juxtaposition of legalism and high levels of public violence that characterizes so many states throughout the hemisphere replicated in their relations with one another. In few other facets of life is the oddly American jumble of distinctiveness, cooperation and resentment clearer. That this is not more often noticed may be put down to cynicism born of an almost visceral resentment. Too often, the public commitment of American states to international law is belittled because it seems belied by poor compliance records in the weaker states and long-running militarized conflicts between them, to say nothing of the fitful unilateralism and periodic interventions of the USA, so nicely captured by one US lawyer a century ago when he wrote that 'Americans [surely meaning his own countrymen] are little

---

[141] In general terms, I follow Hedley Bull, *The Anarchical Society* (London, 1977).

[142] Arie M. Kacowicz, *The Impact of Norms in International Society: the Latin American Experience, 1881–2001* (Notre Dame IN, 2005).

accustomed to consider the feeling of weaker neighbors [and] think diplomacy, especially with weak powers, a kind of solitaire.'[143]

Yet in neither case should imperfection too readily be assumed to be a consequence of hypocrisy. American states have made signal contributions to the development of international law and organization and to the peaceful solution of inter-state conflicts. More than this, their diplomatic expertise, an outcome of European cultural traditions coupled with early political independence, has often secured them a leading role, either singly or collectively, in the development of international law and organization. For its part, the United States was the first state to adopt a formal code based on the just war tradition to govern the conduct of its troops in war. The Lieber Code provided the basis for the army's General Orders No.100 of 1863.[144] It was the United States, too, that took the lead toward the end of the nineteenth century, in a valiant attempt to create a body of American law 'distinct from and superior to the European balance-of-power system' that could provide a model for the development of international law more generally, and which would in due course make a significant contribution to the international order put in place by the United States and its allies after the Second World War.[145]

Much of the inspiration for the project of American law came from the shared founding myth of a New World purged of the corruption of the Old. 'What stronger brotherly relations can be imagined' – asked Venezuelan jurist Andrés Bello (1781–1865) in 1844 – 'than those that link the new American states? When has there existed in the world a group of nations that more truly forms a family?'[146] But the renewal was never complete. A political form of original sin stained the Americas. Witness the larger-than-life-size portrait of a resplendent Bourbon despot, Louis XVI of France, in that holy of holies of the young confederation, Philadelphia's Congress Hall: a token of French assistance mischievously offered and desperately received during the War of Independence. Anglophone and Hispanic America had to fight a second round of independence wars, the former in 1812 and the latter between 1817 and 1824. During the stalemate of 1820–24, before the final crushing victories of Bolívar and José Antonio de Sucre, Spain retained a force some 20,000 strong in the Altiplano

---

[143] Albert Bushnell Hart, 'American Ideals of International Relations,' *American Journal of International Law,* vol. 1, no. 1 (January and April 1907), p. 634.

[144] James Turner Johnson, 'The Just War Idea: the State of the Question,' *Social Philosophy and Policy,* vol. 23, no. 1 (2006), p. 170.

[145] Francis Anthony Boyle, *Foundations of World Order: the Legalist Approach to International Relations (1898–1922)* (Durham NC and London, 1999), p. 103, pp. 1–5 and passim.

[146] Andrés Bello, *Selected Writings of Andrés Bello* (Oxford, 1997), p. 221.

and still aspired to reconquer its American empire with the support of its part-
ners in the Holy Alliance.[147] Brazil, though independent from Portugal after
1822, remained an empire under the Braganzas until 1889. France, as we have
seen, would continue to meddle in the high politics of the hemisphere during
the nineteenth century, as Germany would in the 1930s and Soviet Russia, albeit
on a narrower front, during the Cold War.[148] Such conflicts could never entirely
be isolated from the context of European international politics, which variously
gave rise to or helped shape them. Americans accordingly had at the very least
to take note of relations between the European powers.

It was with precisely such dangers in mind that President James Monroe, in
his 1823 message to Congress, issued the statement for which he is best remem-
bered. The Monroe Doctrine was at first no more than a declaration of policy
by a state with limited ability to enforce it. It would be close to a century before
it acquired formal status as international law, through the Porter Convention of
1907, or credibility, as the United States began to develop armed forces com-
mensurate with its wealth. This said, it unequivocally affirmed that the United
States would not tolerate any fresh European acquisition of territory in the
Western hemisphere by annexation or (through the 1811 No-Transfer
Resolution and the later Polk Corollary) by exchange.

Even the private interests of West European capitalists occasionally prompted
blockades and bombardments, though it was often hard to see what could be
achieved by such means or why petty commercial grievances should be regarded
as matters of state. A British naval officer stationed off Buenos Aires in HMS
Comus in 1845 wrote home disconsolately to say that the only targets he could
identify appeared to belong to his own countrymen. 'You will therefore see how
impossible it is for us to punish the Argentine people without immense loss of
property, and perhaps life too, to ourselves.'[149] The typical Foreign Office reaction to appeals from dispossessed merchants asking for armed intervention on
their behalf was dismissive in the middle decades of the century, unless there was
some complementary consideration of state. There were other fish to fry. Yet
American governments might reasonably doubt whether the United States possessed the military and naval power to deter European intervention south of the

---

[147]   Brading, The First America, pp. 603–8. The Holy Alliance had originally consisted of Austria,
Russia and Prussia in 1815, and was dedicated to the restoration of monarchy and church.
[148]   Stanley E. Hilton , Brazil and the Great Powers, 1930–1939: the Politics of Trade Rivalry (Austin
TX, 1975); Stanley E. Hilton, Hitler's secret War in South America, 1939–1945: German Military
Espionage and Allied Counterespionage in Brazil (Baton Rouge LA, 1981); Christopher Andrew and
Vasili Mitrokhin, The KGB and the World: The Mitrokhin Archive II (London, 2005).
[149]   Kent Archives Office, County Hall, Maidstone, Kent ME14 1XH. Norman MSS, U310
C206/4, Captain T.S. Thompson to G.W. Norman, 27 June 1845.

Caribbean and scarcely dared ignore the ever more interventionist activities of the European powers in Africa and East Asia after 1870. In such circumstances anything that could be done to strengthen legal defences against intervention and establish the inviolability of state sovereignty made good sense. One such initiative was the 1868 suggestion, by Argentine jurist Carlos Calvo (1824–1903), of a standard clause, for inclusion in loan contracts and concessions, accepting that states had no right of intervention provided their own nationals were accorded the same legal rights as the nationals of a host country. In some measure this device succeeded, though the United States demurred, insisting that intervention on behalf of its nationals was legitimate where the level of protection accorded to nationals and non-nationals alike fell below a minimum standard.[150]

Fear of intervention was to reach boiling point at the turn of the twentieth century. The massive display of military force mounted by Britain against two semi-independent Afrikaaner republics worried Argentine statesmen, though as *estancieros* they enjoyed the sharp rise in demand for horses. It is hard to imagine that President Theodore Roosevelt cannot have had these still recent events in mind when, in 1902, following failure to agree on terms of arbitration, a British, Italian and German naval force blockaded the coast of Venezuela in a successful attempt to secure repayment of debts owed by the government of that country to their nationals. The Argentine foreign minister, Luis Drago, responded to the crisis with a letter to the United States administration in which he insisted that the European action breached the Monroe doctrine, noted the imperialist tone of European public opinion, and sought public commitment to the principle 'that the public debt cannot occasion armed intervention nor . . . occupation of the territory of *American* nations by a *European* power'.[151]

Drago got both more and less than he was looking for. The United States responded bullishly with the so-called Roosevelt Corollary to the Monroe Doctrine. This declared that if states in the Western hemisphere failed to maintain civilized standards it was a matter for resolution by Americans, not Europeans. To many in Latin America this looked like a United States offer to act as debt collector for Europe and accept responsibility for dealing with what today we might call failed and murderous states throughout the hemisphere. While United States leadership might be necessary, it was bound to worry less powerful states when it threatened to trample on the principles of sovereign equality and non-intervention. Just such a tendency was evident in an address delivered by former Secretary of State Richard Olney to the American Society of International Law

---

[150] Boyle, *Foundations*, p. 109.

[151] Quoted in H. Edward Nettles, 'The Drago Doctrine in International Law and Politics,' *Hispanic American Historical Review*, vol. 8, no. 2 (1928), at p. 209. My emphases.

in April 1907. Olney advocated a move 'in the direction of qualifying the right of a state to live unto itself alone by insisting upon its rights and duties as a member of the society of states.'[152] And indeed, as the Drago Doctrine passed from a statement of Argentine policy into formal international law following discussion among American states in 1906 and at the Second Hague Peace Conference in 1907, it lost its absolute character, explicitly allowing the use of force in cases where the debtor state had refused arbitration or rejected the outcome of arbitration. The outcome of the whole episode, in short, was that the United States confirmed its hegemonic position in the Americas, while the Argentines failed to advance further those principles of non-intervention and the legal equality of sovereign states that had been their foremost concern.

The Venezuela crisis of 1902–3 merely exposed stresses in inter-American relations that were unavoidable once the United States acquired superior military capability and reputation. Victory in the Spanish-American War of 1898 might have been universally welcomed throughout the hemisphere as a major step forward in the emancipation of the Americas had not Puerto Rico been annexed forthwith by the United States as reparations while the independence long sought for by Cubans was compromised by confrontation between US troops and the home-grown Cuba Libre (Free Cuba) movement and severely qualified by the Platt Amendment to the US Army Appropriation Act of 1901. The United States aroused further suspicions as it conspired to secure the secession of Panama from Colombia in 1903 and began what was to prove a long series of Caribbean interventions by imposing a customs receivership on a chaotic Dominican Republic in 1905.

What is often neglected in the rush to condemn Yankee imperialism is that the United States was very far from being the only aggressor in the Western hemisphere at this time. The reputation of the Americas as a zone of peace is only half deserved.[153] Wars among and within the countries of Central and South America were commonplace during the half-century that followed the abdication of Ferdinand VII in 1808.[154] These struggles centred on state formation. They have already been traced to the highly interdependent character of

---

[152]   Richard Olney, 'The Development of International Law: an address delivered before the American Society of International Law, April 20, 1907' *American Journal of International Law*, vol. 1, no. 1 (January and April 1907), p. 420.

[153]   Arie M. Kacowicz, *Zones of Peace in the Third World: South America and West Africa in Comparative Perspective* (New York NY, 1998); David R. Mares, *Violent Peace: Militarised Interstate Bargaining in Latin America* (New York NY, 2001).

[154]   Miguel Centeno, *Blood and Debt: War and the Nation-State in Latin America* (University Park PA, 2002).

the Spanish fiscal system and their catastrophic economic consequences for Spanish America assessed. Yet this was not the end of it. With the process of national consolidation behind them, some Latin American states began to show expansionist tendencies, resulting in two substantial conflicts in the third quarter of the century and a good deal of arms racing and sabre rattling thereafter. The War of the Triple Alliance (1864–1870) arose from Paraguayan dreams of empire. Ineptitude precipitated the formation of an alliance against Paraguay consisting of Uruguay, Brazil and Argentina. By the end, more than half of the Paraguayan population lay dead. Less bloody, but of great consequence, was the War of the Pacific (1879–1884) in which Chile fought and defeated Bolivia and Peru, making substantial territorial gains and leaving Bolivia landlocked.

Yet all this posturing and the occasional blood-letting it produced were not enough entirely to extinguish more positive and virtually contemporaneous aspects of inter-American relations. As early as 1881, US Secretary of State James Blaine had proposed a conference of American states to consider the prevention of war between them and to consider other ways in which their mutual relations might more readily be governed by law. Ironically, it was war (the War of the Pacific) that delayed this assembly. The First International Conference of American States Washington Conference of 1889–90 was to be the first in a series of ten Pan-American conferences, the last of which took place in 1954. Its most significant achievement was the adoption of a plan for the settlement of disputes between American states by arbitration. A model treaty was drafted, in which arbitration was explicitly referred to as 'a principle of American international law', and though too few states ultimately ratified the treaty for it to enter into force, it was later to provide a model for the Kellogg-Briand pact of 1929, outlawing war generally.[155]

In a summary treatment, these conferences can hardly be taken one by one. Taken together they saw progress in five main areas. The first was the steady institutionalization of cooperation as the early secretariat gave way, in 1910, to a more formal Pan-American Union with a Secretary-General reporting to a governing board chaired by the current United States Secretary of State. A second process was a steady codification of American or inter-American international law as something distinct from international law in general. In a draft declaration of 1925, the American Institute of International Law went so far as to offer a definition of American (not *Latin* American!) international law as 'all of the institutions, principles, rules, doctrines, conventions, customs, and practices which, in the domain of international relations, are proper to the Republics of the new

---

[155] Boyle, *Foundations*, p. 104.

world'.[156] Third came development of the principle of non-intervention, through adoption of the Calvo principle, the subsequent Porter Convention, and final acceptance of the principle by the United States in 1936. A fourth area of activity concerned the legal equality of states, a principle – like non-intervention – formally accepted in 1933 as part of a Convention on the Rights and Duties of States. Last, but not least, the quest for peaceful settlement of disputes that had originally prompted the Pan-American conferences and had already gained wide acceptance in the Americas through a web of bilateral arbitration treaties was further advanced through the 1902 Treaty on Compulsory Arbitration, the 1923 Gondra Treaty, the Saavedra Lamas treaty of 1933 and the system of collective security initiated in 1936 and reinforced through the 1948 Inter-American Treaty on Pacific Settlement and the 1947 Rio Pact, when the possibility of serious European incursion was still a recent memory. Within the much more limited sub-region of Central America, later to prove so troublesome during the closing phase of the Cold War, a regime for the peaceful judicial settlement of disputes was even established in 1907, though it foundered for lack of United States support in 1918.[157]

During the same period, American states were also active in wider international diplomacy, organization and law-making. Ruy Barbosa, the Brazilian delegate, was prominent in discussions at the first Hague Conference of 1899. The United States took steps to ensure that all Latin American states were invited to the second Hague Conference.[158] Ten Latin American states signed the Versailles Treaty as former belligerents following the First World War. These and others joined the League of Nations even though the United States administration failed to win Congressional approval of its own membership. Moreover, the American member states made effective use of caucusing to ensure election of American representatives to key positions, the League representing both an insurance against United States regional hegemony and an opportunity to hone diplomatic and legal skills in a wider arena than the Pan-American conferences and, some might say, without Yankees or Argentines lording it around them.[159] This said, disenchantment set in as the League either ignored American disputes or else deferred to the USA. The Argentines had withdrawn in 1920 when their

---

[156]   Quoted in Hugo Caminos, 'International Law in Latin America or Latin American International Law? Rise, Fall, and Retrieval of a Tradition of Legal Thinking and Political Imagination,' *Proceedings of the American Society for International Law*, vol. 47, no. 1 (Winter 2006). Caminos himself, it should be said, argues cogently against any regional differentiation in the standards and application of international law, preferring to see the Americas as the source of several important legal norms and principles of universal application, including systems of codification (p. 159).

[157]   G. Pope Atkins, *Latin America in the International Political System* (Boulder, 1995), p. 177.

[158]   Peter Calvert, *The International Politics of Latin America* (Manchester, 1994), p. 190

[159]   Calvert, *International Politics*, p. 194.

proposal for universal membership was rejected, only rejoining in 1933. Yet Latin Americans rallied, undismayed, to the internationalist standard when the United Nations Organization was established at the conclusion of the Second World War and have continued, to this day, to make a very substantial contribution to UN military and peacekeeping operations in Korea (1950–63: Colombia and Cuba), Egypt (1956: Brazil and Colombia), Katanga (1961–4: Argentina and Brazil), the Golan Heights (early 1970s: Peru), Cyprus (1993- : Argentina) and the Persian Gulf, where the Argentines patrolled alongside their Canadian and British allies in 1991, enforcing the embargo against Iraq.

Add to all this an emerging twentieth-century pattern of financial missions and development assistance, and the picture that emerges up to 1954 is of a level of regional cooperation in the Americas unparalleled in any other region of the world, facilitated by common culture and lengthy experience of independent statehood and its responsibilities.[160] For a moment it seemed that the post-war period might see a further deepening of cooperation as the Pan-American Union was superseded by the Organization of American States (OAS) with a more elaborate structure and the promise of regular five-yearly conferences. That this did not materialize may in part have been a consequence of United States inattention as confrontation with the Soviet Union in Europe and Asia intensified, casting a Cold War sheen over hemispheric matters that would formerly have been considered in their own right.

Attempting to use the OAS as a Cold War instrument proved self-defeating. A US-sponsored Declaration of Caracas, debated at the 10th Inter-American Conference in 1954, was objected to by many delegates because the United States sought to use it to oppose Communism and justify its unilateral intervention, that very year, against the Leftist Arbenz administration in Guatemala. Mexico and Argentina rejected the Declaration outright, leaving the OAS moribund. The following year saw the creation of the Non-Aligned Movement (NAM), named for the reluctance of its members to take sides in the Cold War. One of the earliest harbingers of cooperation between states of what would soon be known as the Third World, and later the Global South, the NAM originally consisted only of Asian and African states. But after the botched US attempt to reverse Fidel Castro's Cuban Revolution in 1961, the Brazilian military coup of

---

[160] Paul Drake (ed.), *Money Doctors, Foreign Debt and Economic Reform in Latin America from the 1890s to the Present* (Wilmington DE, 1994). It is another small indication of the American problem that this book should contain no essay dealing with the first and – until the 1930s – the most serious financial reconstruction in its chosen period: that which followed the Argentine crisis of 1890, generally known as the Baring crisis. Argentina still seems a long way away from the USA, and in those days was part of a British sphere of influence. Yet why should this continue to govern academic selection?

1964 and the US intervention in the Dominican Republic the following year, Latin American states started to join in substantial numbers. By this time, the NAM was fast becoming just one of a multiplicity of new forums in which Latin America could seek to check growing US hegemony in the Western Hemisphere, many of which, like the United Nations Conference on Trade and Development which first met in 1964, took their developmental nationalist tone from Latin American pioneers, most notably the Argentine economist, Raúl Prebisch. Regulation of international commodity trades, trade in textiles, shipping and nuclear proliferation were among many issues over which Latin Americans, as often allied with non-American states as with one another, would clash with the United States and other wealthy states during the 1970s and 1980s.

It would be a mistake to exaggerate the solidarity of Latin America during the Cold War or the unanimity of its opposition to the United States. Often the so-called North-South dialogue set Latin American states against one another, as when a majority, through UNCTAD, opposed the registration of vessels in 'open register' states, hoping to force them to register at much higher cost in their home countries, and thereby allowing less developed countries to compete more effectively. Clearly this threatened the interests of flag-of-convenience states, such as Panama. Again, the keen interest of Pacific-Coast South American states in the Law of the Sea revived Bolivian resentment at the loss of its Pacific coastline. Conversely, many Latin American states, especially during periods of military government, were resolutely anti-Communist, so much so that they were content to work with the USA. The United States was able to get a two-thirds majority in the OAS in favour of an embargo against Cuba and its exclusion from the organization, though the dissenting minority included the three most populous Latin American states. More substantially, Brazil became a staunch US ally after its 1964 military coup, to the point where some commentators began to write of sub-imperialism during the final decade of the Cold War, as Brazilian generals braced themselves for a final showdown with Cuban Communism in Southern Africa.[161]

The briefest review of four further issues may help bring the story of law-governed international relations and the containment of conflict in the Americas nearer the present and to convey something of the mix of cooperation and polarization, multilateralism and unilateralism, technicality and high politics, good faith and cunning that characterizes the legal culture of the Americas. Law of the Sea, the Antarctic regime, nuclear non-proliferation, and human rights together offer a fair conspectus of this complex field.

---

[161]   Daniel Zirker, 'Brazilian Foreign Policy and Sub-Imperialism during the Political Transition of the 1980s,' *Latin American Perspectives*, vol. 21, no. 1 (Winter, 1994), pp. 115–31.

Law of the Sea

Given the energy with which the United States and other leading maritime states were later to oppose it, there is a certain irony in the fact that it was the proclamation of a United States administration, that of Harry Truman, in September 1945, on the continental shelf and fisheries, that began the move towards a legal norm of 200-mile maritime exclusive economic zones. Truman may have been more concerned about national security and defence against missile-bearing submarines than about natural resources, but his extension of US sovereignty over the deep sea-bed, its subsoil and those fisheries that had customarily been exploited only by US vessels, had great appeal for the governments of Chile, Peru and Ecuador. Faced with unprecedentedly intensive harvesting of tuna and anchovies by United States vessels off their coasts and the possible exhaustion of fish stocks, these three nations laid claim to sovereignty and jurisdiction over sea and seabed resources within 200 nautical miles of their coasts in a series of declarations between 1947 and 1952 and went on to consolidate their various claims to a 200-mile maritime zone in the 1952 Declaration of Santiago. More than this, all three used their innovatory claims to justify arrest of US vessels well beyond the universally recognised 12-mile fisheries zone reserved to coastal states. The United States, for its part, responded by compensating its nationals for their losses out of funds earmarked as aid for the Andean states and went so far, in 1961, as to threaten to debar them entirely from entitlement to development assistance.

Summarizing the position shortly after the third United Nations Conference on Law of the Sea (UNCLOS III) had begun to gather momentum at its 1974 Caracas session, F. V. García-Amador, Director of the OAS Secretariat's Department of Legal Affairs, stopped short of claiming that there was a unified 'Latin American position' on those aspects of the law of the sea that concerned natural resources, but readily conceded that the common tendency of Latin American pronouncements of the preceding thirty years had been toward greater control by coastal states of fisheries and other resources in a much more extensive area than the then established 3-mile band of territorial waters or the 12-mile exclusive fishery zone, before concluding that a consequence of this had been to bring about a more general change of view among developing countries on this subject.[162]

It was indeed no surprise that the 200-mile issue should have become one of the central debating points of UNCLOS III, where a compromise proposal for

---

[162]   F. V. Garcia-Amador, 'The Latin American Contribution to the Development of the Law of the Sea,' *American Journal of International Law*, vol. 68 (1974) p. 50.

exclusive economic zones (EEZ), in which states had rights of resource exploitation and management but not comprehensive sovereign authority, finally won
general acceptance. In spite of United States and United Kingdom rejection of
the final UNCLOS Convention in 1982 and the long subsequent delay in rati-
fication, the 200-mile EEZ had already taken on the status of customary international law embedded, for example, in the common fisheries policy negotiated
by the members of the European Economic Community, including the United
Kingdom, in the 1970s.

Antarctica

If the origins of the 200-mile EEZ give some sense of the blend of legal innovation, sabre-rattling, diplomacy and compromise underlying the emergence of a
new norm and the leadership role of the Americas in this, as in other areas of
emerging international law, then the Antarctic regime provides further evidence
of the irreducibility of international relations to simple North-South oppositions
or, in the Western hemisphere, US confrontation with Latin America. Antarctica,
though of particular concern to Chile and Argentina because of its proximity, was
not solely an American question, since by 1950 the seven states claiming sovereignty in the region included Britain, while several other states with no claims to
sovereignty had nevertheless established scientific research stations. Indeed, the
British claim included the whole of the territory claimed by Argentina and some
of that claimed by Chile, while the claims of the two Southern Cone rivals over-
lapped. Worse, the Chilean geopolitical concept of an 'Arc of the Southern
Antilles' extending westwards from Tierra del Fuego to South Georgia and the
South Sandwich Isles and back again to the tip of the Antarctic Peninsula as the
natural boundary between Atlantic and (Chilean!) Pacific waters made the whole
question contentious in the extreme for Chile and Argentina, and linked it to the
longstanding and complex conflict over the Beagle Channel that was to bring the
two countries to the brink of war in December 1978.

It was therefore a considerable diplomatic achievement, owing much to
United States good offices, for no less than twelve states to sign and subsequently
ratify an Antarctic Treaty in Washington in December 1959. No less than sixty
secret preparatory meetings in Washington had prepared the ground, while the
International Geophysical Year, an eighteen-month non-governmental multidis-
ciplinary and multinational programme of scientific research commencing
in mid-1957, had helped build confidence. The Treaty set agreed limits to the
Antarctic region, prohibited the testing of nuclear weapons and the disposal of
nuclear waste within it and established the basis for cooperative exploration and

scientific research, including agreement on unrestricted access and mutual inspection of all installations. From the restricted point of view of the present study, the salient features of the regime are two. First of all, in spite of the relevance of Antarctic claims to their confrontation with each other, and to the ongoing South Atlantic dispute between Argentina and the United Kingdom, Argentina and Chile found it possible to suspend (but in no way relinquish!) their territorial claims during the life of the treaty. Secondly, at a time when Latin American resentment of the United States was at a high point, in the 1970s and 1980s, both the Southern Cone states resisted the temptation to take up suggestions from the Global South in the 1983 UN General Assembly that Antarctica, on the model of the deep seabed, be regarded as part of the so-called common heritage of humankind, preferring to follow the United States lead and leave well alone.[163]

Nuclear Non-Proliferation

Further evidence of the hemispheric genius for legal innovation and pragmatism is evident in the record on arms control. Once again the themes of North-South tension and geopolitical logic are there. Once again, they are muted. Disarmament, originally thought of within the United Nations Organization as a matter solely for the world's leading military powers, became a more inclusive process when the Disarmament Commission was reconstituted between 1962 and 1969 as the Eighteen Nation Commission on Disarmament, with Brazil and Mexico as members. Argentina became one of the twenty-six members of the expanded UN Committee on Disarmament in 1969. Even before this, Latin American states had been among the signatories to numerous arms control agreements. The most important of these, from an American perspective, was the 1968 Non-Proliferation Treaty by which near-nuclear states relinquished nuclear-weapons in exchange for access to civil nuclear technology developed by the existing nuclear-weapons states. Many Latin American states adhered promptly to the 1968 Treaty, but Argentina and Brazil did not, locked as they were in a military confrontation that would not be resolved until the 1990s.[164] In parallel, the Latin American states negotiated their own regional agreement, the 1968 Treaty of Tlatelolco, making much of the sub-continent a nuclear-free

---

[163] Klaus Dodds, *Geopolitics in Antarctica: Views from the Southern Oceanic Rim* (Chichester, 1997). Arnfinn Jorgensen-Dahl, *et al.*, *The Antarctic Treaty System in World Politics* (London, 1991); Donald Rothwell, *The Polar regions and the development of International Law* (Cambridge, 1966).

[164] Calvert, *International Politics*, pp. 210–12.

zone. These good resolutions only highlighted the real possibility that Southern Cone rivalries might escalate into mutual nuclear deterrence or worse. The characteristically American outcome was that, more through good judgment than good luck, none of the Southern Cone powers moved forward to the production and testing of a nuclear device, no war took place and the rival states achieved lasting détente during the 1980s largely through their own efforts. Argentina, Chile, Brazil finally brought the treaty into force in their territories in 1994. Cuba, which had never after 1962 had any intention of developing such weapons, made the zone complete by ratifying in 2002.

Human Rights

It is sometimes forgotten that these South American accommodations owed as much to the diplomatic efforts of military regimes as to those of their democratic successors. If the tradition of law-governed relations between American states had to weather periods of United States interventionism and geopolitical fantasy, it had also to endure intervals of military rule, too often supported by the United States, in which the most basic rights of Latin American citizens were trampled under foot. The last of the legal regimes considered here, that of human rights, was powerless to prevent these abuses, but its achievements were not negligible and, once again, displayed a distinctively American approach.

As in Europe, so in America, a series of declarations, conventions and institutions have set out to identify and protect human rights. These include the American Declaration of the Rights and Duties of Man (1948), the American Convention on Human Rights (often referred to as the Pact of San José: 1969), and the Inter-American Convention to Prevent and Punish Torture (1985). Less than comprehensive, often merely aspirational, these conventions have allowed for the suspension of rights when they conflict with the general good or in times of national emergency. In short, they are imperfect. Yet the inter-American system protects or aspires to protect a wider range of rights than other regional systems and is in general more restrictive regarding derogations.[165] Moreover, well before the 1969 Convention came into force in 1978, an Inter-American Commission on Human Rights and an Inter-American Court of Human Rights had already been set up under the OAS Charter. The first of these, based in Washington, consisted of seven independent experts appointed for four-year

---

[165] I have relied heavily here on Dinah Shelton, 'The Inter-American Human Rights System,' in Hurst Hannum (ed.), *Guide to International Human Rights Practice*, 2nd ed. (Philadelphia, 1992), pp. 119–32.

terms by the OAS General Assembly. The second was based in San José, Costa Rica, where seven judges, each elected for a six-year term, renewable only once, heard cases prepared by the Commission.

It was easy enough to find fault with this system. The Court could only hear a case if the state concerned was a party to the Convention and had accepted its jurisdiction. By 1992 only 13 of the 35 OAS member-states had taken this second step. As for the Commission, it was poorly financed and under-staffed. The Commissioners themselves were generally part-timers with other posts and responsibilities elsewhere. Yet, ramshackle though it might seem, this apparatus proved able to exert considerable influence without bringing cases to the Court. Crisis intervention by Commissioners was more than once successful. Reports on especially abusive regimes, notably the annual reports on Chile between 1974 and 1980 and the 1979 visit and 1980 report on Argentina, helped mobilize world opinion, the latter prompting a condemnation of the Argentine junta by the government of the United States that almost brought about a break-up of the OAS.[166] Quite different from the European Court of Human Rights, which has generally dealt with detailed points of law and been able to rely on the cooperation of governments, the American system had to work with scant resources, frequently in the face of government obstruction, to combat gross abuses of rights. In doing so, it allowed far more opportunity for petitioners and their representatives to participate in all stages of the legal process and pursued a policy of openness.

To extend the conjunction of public violence and constitutionality characteristic of the domestic politics of American states to their foreign relations is to suggest that American states are peculiarly inclined simultaneously to pursue coercive and legalistic solutions to the conflicts that divide them, and to see no contradiction in this. Thus far, this chapter has dwelt more on the American contribution to international law and organization. From even this briefest of surveys it appears that C. Neale Ronning's 1963 judgment has stood the test of time. Acknowledging that '[t]he vision of an America regulated by its own unique legal order arose with the achievement of independence,' he concluded that the outcome had been 'uncoordinated and confusing' yet insisted, nonetheless, that it had been 'substantial'.[167] In what does that substance consist? More use of arbitration in the long run than elsewhere, less frequent collapse of militarized international disputes into outright war, a thicker texture of regimes

---

[166] A. H. Robertson and J. G. Merrills, *Human Rights in the World; An Introduction to the Study of International Protection of Human Rights*, 4th ed. (Manchester, 1996), pp. 207–8.
[167] C. Neale Ronning, *Law and Politics in Inter-American Diplomacy* (New York and London, 1963), p. 1.

than in any other continent and some leavening of the vast power of the United States and the resentment of its neighbours. Now it is time to look at the occasions when civility in foreign affairs has not been enough, dealing first with military force and then with balancing.

Military Culture

Law, diplomacy and international organization form only part of the machinery of international society. The darker side consists in warfare, great power management (a euphemism for informal imperialism) and the balance of power. As we begin to link together those things that bind the United States to its neighbours and those that set it to one side, matters stand as follows. It was neither religion nor its sublimation in a civic creed that led to the exceptional economic success of the United States. Rather, it was the weakness and lack of sophistication of the British state, which failed to integrate the fiscal system of its empire to the extent that Spain did. Not only did the wars of liberation in Hispanic America retard state consolidation and economic development there; they also resulted in relatively small economies. Meanwhile, the period of disruption to the South was precisely the time when the United States, taking advantage of its larger market and the complex patterns of inter-regional trade that had developed there, found in volume production of labour-saving devices a way of compensating for its shortage of skilled labour that turned out to be a world-beater as the cost of labour rose in other industrialised countries, extending the market for motor vehicles, white goods, and office equipment. This is not the whole of the story. The gargantuan efforts required to win its war against the secessionist South forced an accelerated development of heavy industry in the North and proved that the Union had, should it choose to do so, the capacity to match the established Powers in the forge and on the battlefield.

Even at the outset of the conflict, this was already evident. 'The United States has now created a great army and a great debt,' Trollope observed. 'They will soon also have created a great navy. Affairs of other nations will press upon them, and they will press against the affairs of other nations. In this way statecraft will become necessary to them; and by degrees their ministers will become habile, graceful, adroit – and perhaps crafty, as are the ministers of other nations.'

Here, in that drift toward craftiness, is the moment at which a divergence of capability began to be a divergence of strategy: when the USA began to deviate from American norms. The drift is most evident in the projection of a characteristically American dialectic of law and violence into foreign relations and the modulation of a distinctively American style of warfare.

The first of these two facets of American external relations may best be summed up through the relationship between international law and geopolitics.

We established that it is possible to deploy American evidence to retell the story of international relations, and the academic pursuits based on it, in a way that emphasises the evolution of positive international law and correspondingly de-emphasises the standard text-book account of academic International Relations first rising from the ashes of the First World War.[168] We have seen this played out in Inter-American conferences from the 1880s onward, the codification of American law, later American contributions to international regimes and the creation of distinctive American regimes. Political realists in the United States later misrepresented this promotion of international law as a utopian aberration in response to the First World War. But the extent of United States elite commitment to international law and hemispheric organization before 1917 makes this less convincing than Boyle's view that law provided an economical and indeed a very realist substitution of law for force, ideally suited to the needs of a rising power not yet ready militarily prepared to match the major European states. Instead of appearing to be an outright contradiction of the legal path, breaches of international law in the form of frequent military interventions in the Caribbean basin become, in this version of events, proofs of consistent realism.[169] 'Law when it suits us; force when it doesn't' might be the slogan.

Yet it is not only in the policies of the United States that the paradoxical fusion of legalism and force is to be seen. It may also be detected in other American states. Though international law might, for them far more than for the United States, have been the weapon of choice, this did not rule out occasional use of force.

Latin America has often been regarded as less prone to war than other regions of the world. Yet Argentina, along with its Southern-cone neighbours, Chile and Brazil, has been among the world's great swaggerers over the past century or more, at times acquiring more weaponry of far greater sophistication than it needed or could afford in order to engage in sabre-rattling with its neighbours. Indeed, though many have argued that South America, in particular, is a zone of peace, consistent with the vanguard role of many of its republics in international law and organisation, the converse can be maintained.[170] According to David Mares, levels of conflict in Latin America since independence have *not* been unusually low by comparison with other regions, the Middle East since 1945 excepted.[171]

This should come as no surprise. If one American theme has been a hemisphere of pacific republics, its variations have included the hemisphere-

---

[168]   Boyle, *Foundations of World Order.*
[169]   Boyle, *Foundations.*
[170]   Kacowicz, *Zones of Peace,* p. 68.
[171]   Mares, *Violent Peace,* p. 28.

as-redoubt, the 'Free World' and, latterly, Huntington's 'West' with its fault-line borders and the homeland perimeter, the whole set, taken together, opening the door to mutual suspicions and wars of purification: the hemispheric counterpart of Cold War containment here manifesting once again the hard-edged geography of the New World.[172]

Given this history of sabre-rattling and the predominance of a distinctively modernist view of territoriality in American culture, it is odd to read, in the preface to a North American study of geopolitics in South America, written shortly after and in response to the 1982 Anglo-Argentine conflict in the South Atlantic, of the supposed decline of geopolitical thinking in the United States and the simultaneous eclipse of US influence over Latin American armed forces.[173] It is perfectly true that multilateralist views won out over the earlier isolationist preference of the Roosevelt administration for North-South postwar spheres of influence.[174] But this can hardly be said to be the end of the story. Isolationism did not simply evaporate, and multilateralism was by no means an unambiguously liberal policy. Indeed, at the moment of its triumph Nicholas Spykman's influential study, *America's Strategy in World Politics* was providing a thoroughly realist justification for multilateralism based on the unsustainability of the Western hemisphere in isolation.[175]

Spykman's study has two salient characteristics. The first is an evident debt to the German tradition of geopolitics, which marks it off from the fleeting liberal multilateralism of the mid-1940s but links it to South American thinking and to an important strand of strategic thought in the United States itself during the Cold War. For the Communist threat, understood in geopolitical terms, was a threat to dominate the world through control of the Eurasian heartland, and because it was perceived in precisely these terms, local conflicts on the edge of the heartland – in the so-called rimlands – took on a supposed significance they might otherwise have lacked: Korea, Vietnam, Palestine, Germany.[176]

---

[172] On the development of United States concepts of territoriality see John Rennie Short, *Representing the Republic: Mapping the United States, 1600–1900* (London, 2001).

[173] Jack Child, *Geopolitics and Conflict in South America: Quarrels Among Neighbors* (New York, 1985), p. ix.

[174] The tendency of US policy, whether hemispheric and isolationist or United Nations and multilateralist, was the subject of constant speculation within the British diplomatic service and the Foreign Office in 1942–43. FO371 30503, 33900, 33901, 33902, 33803, and 33903 give a good flavour of this debate.

[175] Nicholas John Spykman, *America's Strategy in World Politics: the United States and the Balance of Power* (New York, 1942).

[176] James E. Dougherty and Robert L. Pfaltzgraff, Jr., *Contending Theories of International Relations: a Comprehensive Survey,* 3rd ed. (New York, 1990), p. 63: '[W]riters such as Nicholas J. Spykman

The second striking feature of Spykman's book is a mercantilist preoccupation with logistics and the security of resources that anticipates the rise of international political economy in the 1970s, following the first oil crisis and the collapse of Bretton Woods. In a neglected work that wonderfully anticipated (and solved) the 1973–4 oil crisis in a couple of lucid pages, Mancur Olson contrasted the liberalism of Britain in three world wars with the mercantilism of its chief opponents. Britain had survived, he argued, because the flexibility of the economy allowed it to respond rapidly and completely enough to mount an effective defence following the outbreak of war, thereby avoiding the cost to its economy of sustained preparation for war in time of peace. Were the price of oil to double overnight, he suggested, liberal economies would rapidly (if a little painfully) adjust through substitution and development of fresh supplies. Better this than expensive preparation for a day that might never come, he maintained. Yet the Cold War stockpiling policies of the United States, as much as the import-substituting industrialization policies of its southern neighbours perhaps betokened a greater concern at the margin about strategic exposure in the Americas than was to be found in Europe, where the social exposure that motivated European agricultural subsidies was paramount.[177] (European fear of class struggle needs to be distinguished from American fear of racial conflict. Here, as elsewhere, the further East in Europe, the more 'American'.)

As for an eclipse of United States influence over the military establishments of South America in the 1960s and 70s, this sits ill with what we know of US training and funding during the dirty wars of the 1970s and into the last phase of the Cold War in the 1980s, not least through the United States Army's School of the Americas, first at Fort Bragg, North Carolina, and latterly at Fort Benning, Georgia.[178]

If geopolitical and mercantilist thought in the Americas accounts for the persistence of conflict, especially in the more divided South, the more fundamental problem with application of the democratic peace approach to the Americas

---

... suggested that the "rimland" of Eurasia might prove strategically more important than the Heartland if new centers of industrial power and communications were created along the circumference of the Eurasian land mass. The "rimland" hypothesis is a central theoretical foundation of George F. Kennan's famous proposal for a "policy of containment" of the Soviet Union, which became the philosophical basis for the American foreign policy of internationalism beginning with the Truman Doctrine and the Marshall Plan in 1947.'

[177] Mancur Olson, *The Economics of Wartime Shortage: a History of British Food Supplies in the Napoleonic War and World Wars I and II* (Durham NC, 1963).

[178] Lesley Gill, *The School of the Americas: Military Training and Political Violence in the Americas* (Durham NC and London, 2004). See also Robert H. Holden, *Armies Without Nations: Public Violence and State Formation in Central America, 1821–1960* (Oxford, 2004).

resides in the development of a distinctive American way of war which has gone unrecorded by scholars working in the correlates of war tradition.[179] The standard definition recognizes as wars only such struggles between internationally recognised states as result in more than a minimal number of battle deaths. Mares starts to challenge this through a discussion of 'militarised disputes', not all of which meet the criteria for war proper.

A less direct yet perhaps more subversive challenge has now been mounted by a clutch of authors of disparate political views, including John Grenier, Fred Anderson, and Max Boot.[180] Grenier believes the standard view on United States strategy to have been excessively concerned with the military operations of federal forces beyond the country's borders. To include the military operations of forces raised or supported by individual states in wars of conquest in North America, he argues, is to discover a world in which irregular and unlimited warfare were commonplace. Once the view of United States military culture is adjusted for this, aspects of military history that once seemed exceptional or aberrant begin to fall into place. Those who accept the orthodox view of United States military history will dismiss My Lai as an anomaly. Instead, Grenier presents it as 'a grim waypoint in the evolution of the American way of war.' Systematic violence against civilians, he argues, has been part of American warfare from the start.[181]

From this, two corollaries may be derived. Firstly, United States military culture may turn out to have been less exceptional and more like the military culture of other American states than has generally been admitted. Secondly, the militarized conflicts of Mares's book – sustained low-level encounters, occasionally flaring – can less easily be dismissed from the record once the 'first way of war' is admitted to be central to US military culture. This, in turn, would bring into the calculations of the inductivists historical conflicts between Latin American polities that are currently excluded – some of them between constitutional if not wholly democratic regimes – while also posing the problem of the solution of some of these (that between Argentina and Chile after 1978, for example) by wholly undemocratic dyads.[182]

---

[179] A good sense of the 'Correlates of War' approach can be had from John A. Vasquez and Marie T. Henehan, *The Scientific Study of Peace and War: a Text Reader* (New York, 1992). For the operational definition of war, see pp. 384ff. Note, p. 385: 'Since we are mainly interested in the larger and more modern entities and the wars they fight (*sic*), it makes sense to exclude from our study of war tribes of American Indians, for example, even through this certainly does not mean we consider the deaths of American Indians less significant or regrettable.'

[180] Grenier, *The First Way of War*.

[181] Grenier, *First Way of War*, p. 224. See also Fred Anderson and Andrew Cayton, *The Dominion of War: Empire and Conflict in America, 1500–2000* (London, 2005).

[182] Gian Luca Gardini ' Democracy and Regionalisation in the Southern Cone: Relations between Argentina and Brazil, 1979–1991' (Unpublished Doctoral Dissertation, Cambridge UK, 2005).

Correlative or inductivist work on the democratic peace claims that democracies do not fight one another; it does not claim that democracies are disinclined to fight undemocratic polities or that they are, in a general way, peaceable. Yet explanations of the infrequency of war between democracies tend to attach value to liberalism, or republicanism, or democracy (it is often unclear quite which is doing the work), so the admission of irregular and asymmetric conflicts, and their solution, not only threatens the neatness of the correlations but also sows seeds of doubt about conventional explanations of them.[183]

Balancing Failure

One final feature of international relations in the Americas might seem to be the failure of regional balancing. If, as many political scientists have argued, balancing against an emergent hegemon is the universal norm in international relations, then how on earth did the United States get so out of hand? With the presence of other European powers in the Americas much diminished by 1825, the British could be forgiven for passing up Texas and the Pacific coast, and allowing their empire to tilt finally and decisively to the East in the middle decades of the nineteenth century. The leading concerns of the British state over the following century were to be the Eastern Question and the security of the Indian Empire and, only later, the consolidation of Central European states.[184] British trade was becoming steadily more dependent on continental Europe for its imports between 1850 (37 per cent) and 1890 (46 per cent).[185] Strategy and commerce both supported the turn to Asia and the Mediterranean, however unpleasant its consequences might be for the complexion of domestic politics. Yet the foreseeable consequence was that if the United States of America could only hold together – still more confederation than federation – it would sooner or later become a major hemispheric and world power.[186] Commentators as different as

---

[183]   The explanatory literature built on the democratic peace generalisation is vast. For some sense of it see Bruce Russett, *Grasping the Democratic Peace: Principles for a Post-Cold War World* (Princeton, NJ,1993), Nicholas G. Onuf and Thomas J. Johnson, 'Peace in the Liberal World: Does Democracy Matter?' in Charles W. Kegley, Jr. (ed.), *Controversies in International Relations Theory: Realism and the Neoliberal Challenge* (New York, 1995) and Tarak Barkawi and Mark Laffey (eds.), *Democracy, Liberalism, and War* (Boulder, CO and London, 2001).

[184]   Even then, it was Italy that worried many British policy makers more than Germany because of its position in the Mediterranean. See E.H. Carr, 'Great Britain as a Mediterranean Power' Cust Foundation Lecture, University College, Nottingham, 1937 (Nottingham, 1937).

[185]   Jones, *El reino unido y américa*.

[186]   Daniel Deudney, 'The Philadelphia System: Sovereignty, Arms Control and Balance of Power in the American States-Union, circa 1787–1861,' *International Organization*, vol. 49, no. 2 (1995), pp. 191–228.

Cobden and de Tocqueville were agreed upon this, and the only American states that have ever seemed capable of challenging US supremacy, Argentina and Brazil, have never come close.[187]

Traditional International Relations scholarship, committed to balancing as a systemic norm, might regard the lack of a regional balance of power system in the Americas as exceptional. It might be accounted for by the combination of luck and skill that eliminated European powers, one by one, from the hemisphere and focused their attention upon one another. Alternatively it might be disregarded as a local consequence of the logic of US participation in a great power system, first multipolar, then bipolar, and finally unipolar. A more recent view, based on extensive investigation of states-systems over the past three millennia and more consistent with older views in political sociology, suggests that it is the modern European experience of balancing, with its transitory global expansion, that has been the exception, and great power or imperial management of extensive coteries of culturally homogenous polities the norm.[188]

For the republics to the South (Canada being in this, as so much else, the great exception) a hegemonic United States has been variously interpreted as the beneficent provider of security, currency and credit or else the arch-exploiter and bully. Such is the fate of all imperial powers; and the last point to make about the distinctiveness of international relations in the Americas is, bluntly, that they have long been imperial in a way that world politics are only now, and haltingly, becoming imperial.

---

[187]   De Tocqueville's views are well known: *Democracy in America* (various editions), Cobden's less so. He wrote to his fellow Radical, John Bright, on 8th September 1863, that while some British aristocrats had welcomed the outbreak of the American Civil War as a defeat of republicanism, he felt, by contrast, that 'the experience of the last two years shows that whether in peace or war, this Republic, instead of a bubble, is the greatest and most solid fact in all history'. Quoted in John Morley, *The Life of Richard Cobden* [1879] (London, 1905), p. 878. The relative decline of Argentina makes the idea of its hegemony within the Southern Cone so implausible today that one must go back half a century to read an account, written from a Northern American perspective, that takes this prospect seriously (and helps account for the strength of US reaction against Argentina in the later 1940s). See Olive Holmes, 'Argentina and the Dream of Southern Union,' in *Political, Economic, and Social Problems of the Latin-American Nations of Southern South America: Papers Read in a Lecture Series Dealing with Political, Economic, and Social Problems of the Latin-American Nations of Southern South America*, Austin, Texas, 1948 (New York, 1948), pp. 43–57. See also Callum McDonald, 'The United States, Great Britain and Argentina in the Years Immediately after the Second World War,' in Guido di Tella and D.C.M. Platt (eds.), *The Political Economy of Argentina, 1880–1946* (Basingstoke, 1986)

[188]   William H. Wohlforth et al. 'Testing Balance-of-Power Theory in World History,' *European Journal of International Relations*, vol. 13, no. 2 (June, 2007), pp. 155–185; E.L. Jones, *The European Miracle: Environments, Economies, and Geopolitics in the History of Europe and Asia* (Cambridge, 1981).

It is helpful to distinguish here between formal and informal empire on the one hand, and direct and indirect rule on the other. In a relationship of informal empire, the influence upon a nominally autonomous subject state of interests, organizations, and regimes controlled from outside its borders is so strong as to substantially circumscribe the options open to its government. In formal empire, the subject state explicitly acknowledges the supreme military power and legal authority of the imperial state. Yet this closer relationship leaves open the question of government, which may be either direct or indirect. In the former, metropolitan law, education, and administration is imposed on the subject state; in the latter, local authorities are left in place to run the country in the customary manner, provided only that they provide resources for the maintenance and defence of the empire as a whole.

There is nothing new in the suggestion that the United States is an imperial power, though many still strongly deny this.[189] It used to be said that US imperialism was distinguished from recent European imperialisms by its informality. But given that the essence of imperialism is military power and ultimate judicial authority rather than administration, it may be more accurate to regard the contemporary US empire as *formal*, by virtue of its repeated use of public violence, its interventions, and its occupations, but almost always *indirect*. What can easily be missed by the casual European observer, to whom the interventions of 1917 and 1943 may appear benevolent and the treatment of German enemies, once defeated, remarkably lenient, is that the record of the United States elsewhere has been consistently less amicable.

In a manner reminiscent of the pre-Columbian Aztec and Inca tribute-empires, the United States has generally offered a seemingly balanced and reciprocal deal in which states voluntarily coming within its sphere of influence gain economically and receive enhanced security.[190] But an empire of this sort, formal yet indirect, requires occasional displays of extreme force – a Hiroshima here, a Fallujah there – their effectiveness as demonstrations being almost proportionate to their excess and seeming inappropriateness to local and specific circumstances. Europe was not the place in 1945; the target was insufficiently isolated, the Soviets too close in every sense. Japan perfectly served the purpose,

---

[189] See, for example, Andrew J. Bacevich, *American Empire: The Realities and Consequences of U.S. Diplomacy* (Cambridge MA, 2002).

[190] For the pre-Columbian precedents see Ross Hassig, *War and Society in Ancient Mesoamerica* (Berkeley CA, 1992), pp. 137 and 145–6; Joseph Bram, *An Analysis of Inca Militarism* (New York, 1941), p. 137; Pedro Carrasco, *The Tenochca Empire of Ancient Mexico: the Triple Alliance of Tenochtitlan, Tetxcoco, and Tlapcopan* (Norman OK, 1999); Herbert S. Klein, *A Concise History of Bolivia* (Cambridge, 2003), pp. 19–20; María Rosworowski de Díez Canseco, *History of the Inca Realm* (Cambridge, 1999), p. 223.

whether intentionally or not. Korea did not entirely fit the bill, but the campaign in Vietnam, even as it lurched toward defeat, made the point through its reliance upon and subsequent mythologizing of profligate destruction. The first Gulf War of 1991 would not serve: too obviously a just and legal response to a clear wrong committed by Iraq against Kuwait; but the second Iraq war: pre-emptive, illegal, immoral, *and* imprudent was, precisely for this reason, entirely rational.

Americans know this. At the hands of the United States, the republics have for more than a century experienced the surreal blend of Quixotic legalism, 'assistance' and cooperation, punctuated by sudden and extreme use of force. Sometimes this has been public, sometimes (bizarrely) private; sometimes explicit and sometimes clandestine. Yet throughout it has been consistently inconsistent, rationally irrational. And in imperial politics of this sort, it is not the power of one's state or the ability to build a coalition that matters, for neither can match the hegemon, but rather the extent of one's access to court. So President Batlle of Uruguay was known to gain purchase by arranging to be conspicuously called away from a meeting of his South American peers to receive a call from the White House. So Vicente Fox relished being the first Latin American president to meet with George W. Bush. So Tony Blair . . . while the French, still living in a different and a better world, though hardly a real one, persist in their reliance on principle, sovereignty, diplomacy, and law. In a world that is becoming daily more American it is well to know just what being American entails.

CHAPTER V

American Civilization

The purpose of this extended essay has been to sketch the outlines of an American civilization and, by implication, to suggest a cultural division between Western Europe and those countries in which European colonies most completely succeeded in eliminating or dominating indigenous and enslaved populations. This might easily seem like a recasting of the familiar thesis of a clash of civilizations. In Samuel Huntington's formulation Mexico and Turkey were cast as 'torn' countries, the former caught between Latin America and the West, the latter between the West and Islam. In the revised version it might seem that the United States is to figure as a country torn between Europe and America, leaning more than any other American state toward European manners and style, especially in military culture and the practice of *real politik*. Conversely, Britain rather than Turkey would appear as the torn country of Europe: leaning toward America, by turns anti-European or desperate to join in, but always on its own terms.

To argue along these lines would be to mistake the very concept of civilization in play here, which is not that of Huntington. Many approaches to the study of America have ultimately depended on the extension, north or south, of some mono-causal explanation, or consist more modestly in the study of commonalities and variations in some specific feature common to societies throughout the continent. The approach that has been taken here is a little more complicated, for the argument has not consisted simply in a set of generalisations: that the United States or the Americas in general are more or less legalistic or violent or racist or materialist than European states. All these claims have been made at one time or another. Each falls short of the mark. Instead, what is suggested here is that debates in the Americas about modernity, economy and civility have followed courses and flowed within quite generously set limits that are distinctively American.

Modernity has been a global and multi-centred phenomenon. The claim is not that the distinctive American generation and experience of modernity can be established by ascertaining the values of a half-dozen variables. It is that the range and patterns of national variation in the Americas between imitation, tradition, innovation and revolution bear strong family resemblances. It is not that the Americas have been, say, more protectionist or more liberal than European states, but that the ways in which the environment, labour, and political economy have been perceived and the discourses flowing from these perceptions have a peculiarly American flavour. It is not that Americans, North and South, are any more or less civil or violent than Europeans, but that the complex relations between public violence, political constitution, citizenship and the rule of law that obtain in the Americas have a style of their own that is distinguishable from the equally diverse set of relations that constitutes European political life.

The fact that all these countries – however different one from another – are creole states established in more or less conscious reaction against a European states-system defined by heredity and the balance of power and in defiance of more or less substantial populations of indigenous and African-American non-citizens has made them profoundly different from France, Britain, Spain or Portugal. This is not a study of contemporary foreign policy, but it is suggested that these distinctively American dialogues have had strong implications for the ways in which American states have related to one another and to the rest of the world, and these implications, in turn, have taken on global significance in recent years because of the pre-eminence of the United States following the collapse of the Soviet Union. The central argument, then, is that a discernibly American identity, nonetheless real for having been so long obscured by the possibly fleeting preponderance of the USA, unites the republics of the Western hemisphere in the modern period and, together with variations in capacity and circumstance, helps delineate the range of their behaviour toward one another and toward states elsewhere.

A definition of civilization consistent with this analysis is not concerned to establish homogeneity within a territory with clearly defined borders, but to recognise a distinctive style of interaction, and above all a distinctive solution to the challenge of cultural difference within a territory. The relational view of civilization I have proposed applies finally to concepts of territoriality, which for the modernist, are dominated by consistency, containment and contiguity. A post-modern concept of territoriality is more concerned with nodes, networks, projects and processes. Since it is most often in metropolitan cities that the problem of difference appears in its most acute form, the style of a civilization is most often dictated by the solutions found there: in Peking, in Rome, in London, in New York or in Rio de Janeiro.

The problem of difference exists in every major city, and when a solution developed in one city spreads throughout the whole of an extensive culture, often but not necessarily as a consequence of empire, we speak of a civilization. But viewed this way, an empire is most itself in its cities and at its core. Viewed Huntington's way, it is most itself at the frontier.

This is not helpful, because no frontier can be drawn around Islam or Christianity or any other world religion, let alone around the powerful process of material acculturation, in large part American, which we call globalization. It is most of all in the world's great cities that different religions, different ethnic groups, traditional and post-modern life-styles live cheek by jowl.

Solutions that rely on internal frontiers are no solutions at all. The kind of multi-culturalism that sets out to encourage good community relations by first essentialising communities amounts to a ghetto of the mind and is almost as pernicious in its long-run effects as the literal ghettoes that used to exist in European cities or the modern practice of addressing ethnic conflict by partition: of Ireland, of British India, of Bosnia. But where Huntington opts for assimilation as a solution to this dilemma, I favour a more eclectic approach to interaction that tolerates difference within as well as between individuals.

Like Huntington I am a social constructivist, believing that we make our own social world by our actions and that, by embedding our practices and values in institutions we create structures that constrain the agency of those who follow us. However Huntington's social constructivism is a much more monumental business than mine. It might even be called tombstone constructivism. The American creed came into being through historical contingency but it followed a clear blueprint and, once in place on the family plot, has weighed down on the nation's chest, inhibiting further political development. By contrast, mine is shanty-town constructivism – a slash and burn constructivism, in which the process of construction is incessant, piecemeal and shifting.

I repeat. This is not a study of contemporary foreign policy. It is left to the reader to draw detailed implications. Yet one thing needs to be made clear. When the United States acts unilaterally, when it uses force, when it breaches the law, when it offends half of humankind, it is not acting as any other country with its military and material advantages would act. If the development of an American civilization means anything, it means that the muddle of oil lobbies and democratization, religiosity and republicanism, civility and violence that characterised United States grand strategy is symptomatic of its American character, not simply of its supremacy. Russia would have acted differently. China has, and will.

One conclusion that follows from all this is that Huntington has been mistaken in his lurch into nationalism and isolationism. People constantly speak of

China or India as the power of the future. But the clever money should be on America: not the USA, but America. As Felipe Fernández-Arnesto put it: 'If the twentieth century was "American" by virtue of US predominance, the twenty-first may be American too, in a fuller sense of the word.'[191] Neo-conservatism, cosmopolitanism and nationalism do not exhaust the US foreign policy repertoire. A more balanced engagement, with America as the foundation of a continuing US global role, is not impossible even though it looks so at present because of the obsessions and negligence of this administration and its immediate predecessors, distracted first by the break-up of the Soviet empire and then by the spectre of global terrorism.

A political solution is possible in Colombia and was on the cards until 9/11 knocked the US off course and sidelined Colin Powell's diplomacy. A transition will take place before long in Cuba in which the United States can play a constructive role if it chooses. Populism fed by high commodity prices need not translate into enduring Chinese political influence and will melt away if Asian development falters. Continuing normal economic relations between Venezuela and the USA belie the wilder populist flourishes of Hugo Chavez. Elsewhere pragmatists may be posing as populists this year, but they can turn at the merest hint of a more constructive style of engagement in Washington. It is to be hoped that the clearer sense of kinship and common purpose that comes with the idea of American civilization may help a recovery of good relations in the hemisphere and that a more civilized America may help the rest of us.

---

[191]   Fernández-Arnesto, *The Americas*, p. 132.

BIBLIOGRAPHY

Abrams, Robert E. (2004) *Landscape and Ideology in American Renaissance Literature: Topographies of Skepticism* (Cambridge: Cambridge University Press).

Adler, Dorothy B. (1970) *British Investment in American Railways, 1934–1898* (Charlottesville, VA: University Press of Virginia).

Alberdi, Juan Bautista (1913) *The Crime of War* [1870] (London: Dent).

Albion, Robert Greenhalgh (1939) *The Rise of New York Port, 1815–1860* (New York: Scribner's Sons).

Anderson, Fred (2001) *Crucible of War: the Seven Years' War and the Fate of Empire in British North America, 1754–1766* (London: Faber & Faber).

Anderson, Fred, and Andrew Cayton (2005) *The Dominion of War: Empire and Conflict in America, 1500–2000* (London: Atlantic Books).

Anderson, Robert Nelson (1996) 'The *Quilimbo* of Palmares: a New Overview of a Maroon State in Seventeenth-Century Brazil,' *Journal of Latin American Studies*, vol. 28, no. 3 (October), pp. 545–566.

Andrew, Christopher and Vasili Mitrokhin (2005) *The KGB and the World: the Mitrokhin Archive II* (London: Allen Lane).

Andrews, Alice C., and James W. Fonseca (1995) *The Atlas of American Society* (New York & London: New York University Press).

Arendt, Hannah (1973) *On Revolution* (Harmondsworth: Penguin).

Bacevich, Andrew J. (2002) *American Empire: The Realities and Consequences of U.S. Diplomacy* (Cambridge, MA: Harvard University Press)

Baechler, Jean (1975) *The Origins of Capitalism* (Oxford: Palgrave Macmillan).

Barkawi, Tarak, and Mark Laffey (eds.) (2001) *Democracy, Liberalism, and War* (Boulder, CO and London: Lynne Rienner).

Barraclough, Geoffrey (1967) *An Introduction to Contemporary History* (Harmondsworth: Penguin).

Baudrillard, Jean (1988) *America* (London and New York: Verso).

Bayly, C.A. (2004) *The Birth of the Modern World, 1780–1914: Global Connections and Comparisons* (Oxford: Blackwell).

Bellesiles, Michael A. (2000) *Arming America: the Origins of a National Gun Culture* (New York: Alfred A. Knopf).

Bello, Andrés (1997) *Selected Writings of Andrés Bello* (London: Oxford University Press).

Bolton, Herbert Eugene (1933) 'The Epic of Greater America,' *American Historical Review*, vol. 38, no. 3 (April 1933), pp. 448–74.

Boyle, Francis A. (1999) *Foundations of World Order: the legalist approach to international relations, 1898–1922* (Durham, NC and London: Duke University Press).

Brading, D.A. (1991) *The First America: the Spanish Monarchy, Creole Patriots, and the Liberal State, 1492–1866* (Cambridge: Cambridge University Press).

Bram, Joseph (1941) *An Analysis of Inca Militarism* (New York: J. J. Augustin).

Brand, Stewart (1995) *How Buildings Learn: What Happens After They're Built* (New York &c: Penguin Books).

Brassey, Thomas (1886–) *The Naval Annual* (Portsmouth: Griffin & Co.).

Brooks, Philip C. (1952) 'Do the Americas Share a Common History?' *Revista de historia de América*, no. 33 (1952), pp. 75–83.

Brown, George W. (1942) 'A Canadian View,' *Canadian Historical Review*, vol. 23, pp. 132–8.

Brown, R. Craig (1964) *Canada's National Policy, 1883–1900: a Study in Canadian-American Relations* (Princeton, NJ: Princeton University Press).

Bull, Hedley (1977) *The Anarchical Society* (London: Macmillan).

Cain, Peter (1979) 'Capitalism, War and Internationalism in the Thought of Richard Cobden,' *British Journal of International Studies*, vol. 5, no. 3 (October), pp. 229–247.

Callahan, John F. (1997) 'Lynching' in William L. Andrews, Frances Smith Foster and Trudier Harris (eds.) *The Oxford Companion to African American Literature* (New York and Oxford: Oxford University Press) pp. 465–7.

Calvert, Peter (1994) *The International Politics of Latin America* (Manchester: Manchester University Press).

Caminos, Hugo (2006) 'International Law in Latin America or Latin American International Law? Rise, Fall, and Retrieval of a Tradition of Legal Thinking and Political Imagination,' *Proceedings of the American Society for International Law*, vol. 47, no. 1 (Winter 2006), pp. 283–305

Carr, E.H. (1937) 'Great Britain as a Mediterranean Power' Cust Foundation Lecture, University College, Nottingham, 1937 (Nottingham: Published by the University).

Carrasco, Pedro (1999) *The Tenochca Empire of Ancient Mexico: the Triple Alliance of Tenochtitlan, Tetxcoco, and Tlapcopan* (Norman, OK: University of Oklahoma Press).

Centeno, Miguel (2002) *Blood and Debt: War and the Nation-State in Latin America* (University Park, PA: Pennsylvania University Press).

Chaowsangrat, Chaowarit (n.d.) 'Comparative Trends in Violent Crime: the Latin American Context,' cited in L Piquet Carneiro 'Violent Crime in Latin American Cities: Rio de J and Sao P' (Washington DC 2000), at p.26 and accessed at http://www.cerac.org.co).

Child, Jack (1985) *Geopolitics and Conflict in South America: Quarrels Among Neighbors* (New York &c: Praeger).

Cicerchia, Ricardo (2004) 'Journey to the Centre of the Earth,' *Journal of Latin American Studies*, vol. 36, no. 2 (May), pp. 205–232.

Churchill, Ward (1997) *A Little Matter of Genocide: Holocaust and Denial in the Americas, 1492 to the Present* (San Francisco, CA: City Lights Books).

Clements, Roger V. (1955) 'The Farmers' Attitude toward British Direct Investment in American Industry,' *Journal of Economic History*, vol. 15, no. 2, pp. 151–9.

Coatsworth, John H. (1998) 'Economic and Institutional Trajectories in Nineteenth-Century Latin America,' in John H. Coatsworth and Alan M. Taylor (eds.) *Latin America and the World Economy since 1800* (Cambridge, MA: Harvard University Press for the David Rockefeller Center for Latin American Studies).

Coatsworth, John H. and Jeffrey G. Williamson (2004) 'Always Protectionist? Latin American Tariffs from Independence to Great Depression,' *Journal of Latin American Studies*, vol. 36, no. 2, pp. 205–232.

Cooper, James Fennimore (1992) *The Last of the Mohicans*. [1826] (London: Penguin).

Crapol, Edward P. (1973) *America for American: Economic Nationalism and Anglophobia in the Late Nineteenth Century* (Westport, CO: Greenwood Press).

Creighton, D. G. (1937) 'The Economic Background of the Rebellions of 1837,' *Canadian Journal of Economic and Political Science*, vol. 3, no. 3 (August), pp. 322–334.

Cunha, Euclides da (1995) *Rebellion in the Backlands* [1902: trans. University of Chicago Press, 1944] (London: Picador).

Davis, Lance E. and Douglass C. North (1971) *Institutional Change and American Economic Growth* (Cambridge: Cambridge University Press).

Deudney, Daniel H. (1995) 'The Philadelphia System: Sovereignty, Arms Control and Balance of Power in the American States-Union, circa 1787–1861,' *International Organization*, vol. 49, no. 2 (Spring) pp. 191–228.

Dodds, Klaus (1997) *Geopolitics in Antarctica: Views from the Southern Oceanic Rim* (Chichester: Wiley in association with the Scott Polar Research Institute, Cambridge).

Dougherty, James E., and Robert L. Pfaltzgraff, Jr. (1990) *Contending Theories of International Relations: a Comprehensive Survey* (3rd ed. New York: Harper & Row).

Drake, Paul W. (ed.) (1994) *Money Doctors, Foreign Debt and Economic Reform in Latin America from the 1890s to the Present* (Wilmington, DE: SR Books).

Dressing, J. David (1996) 'Latin America,' in Barbara A. Tennebaum (ed.) *Encyclopedia of Latin American History and Culture* (New York: Scribner's Sons).

Dubois, Laurent (2004) *Avengers of the New World* (Cambridge, MA: Harvard University Press.

Dunkerley, James (2000) *Americana: The Americas in the World around 1850* (London: Verso).

Dye, Richard (1998) *Cuban Sugar in the Age of Mass Production: Technology and the Economics of the Sugar Central, 1899–1929* (Stanford, CA: Stanford University Press).

Edgerton, David (2007) 'Slower Technology,' *Prospect*, vol. 13.

Elliott, J.H. (2006) *Empires of the Atlantic World: Britain and Spain in America, 1492–1830* (New Haven, CT and London: Yale University Press).

Encina, Francisco A. (1986), *Nuestra Inferioridad Económica* [1911] (Santiago de Chile: Editorial Universitaria).

Etherington, Norman (1984) *Theories of Imperialism: War, Conquest and Capital* (London: Croom Helm).

Fernández-Arnesto, Felipe (2003) *The Americas: the History of a Hemisphere* (London: Phoenix).

Fernández-Santamaría, J.A. (1977) *The State, War and Peace: Spanish Political Thought in the Renaissance, 1516–1559* (Cambridge: Cambridge University Press).

Ferns, Harry S. (1973) *The Argentine Economy, 1516–1971* (Newton Abbot: David & Charles).

Foote, Nicola (2006) 'Race, State and Nation in Early Twentieth Century Ecuador,' *Nations and Nationalism*, vol. 12, no. 2 (April), pp. 261–278.

Fowke, V. C. (1952) 'The National Policy, Old and New,' *Canadian Journal of Economics and Political Science*, vol. 18, no. 3 (August).

Frank, Andre Gunder (1969) *Latin America: Underdevelopment or Revolution. Essays on the Development of Underdevelopment and the Immediate Enemy* (New York: Monthly Review Press).

Friede, Juan, and Benjamin Keen (eds.) (1971) *Bartolomé de las Casas: Toward an Understanding of the Man and his Work* (DeKalb, IL: Northern Illinois Press).

Garcia-Amador, F. V. (1974) 'The Latin American Contribution to the Development of the Law of the Sea,' *American Journal of International Law* vol. 68, no. 1 (January), pp. 33–50.

Gardini, Gian Luca (2005) ' Democracy and Regionalisation in the Southern Cone: Relations between Argentina and Brazil, 1979–1991' (Cambridge: unpublished doctoral dissertation).

Gilbert, Geoffrey (2001) *World Population: A Reference Handbook* (Santa Barbara, CA: AB Clio).

Gilje, Paul J. (1996) *Rioting in America* (Bloomington & Indianapolis IN: Indiana University Press).

Gill, Lesley (2004) *The School of the Americas: Military Training and Political Violence in the Americas* (Durham, NC and London: Duke University Press).

Goodwin, D. W. (1961) *Canadian Economic Thought: The Political Economy of a Developing Nation, 1814–1914* (Durham, NC: Duke University Press).

Gootenberg, Paul (1999) 'Reluctance or Resistance? – Constructing Cocaine (Prohibitions) in Peru, 1910–1950,' in Paul Gootenberg (ed.) *Cocaine: Global Histories* (London: Routledge), pp. 46–79.

Grafe, Regina, and Maria Alejandra Irigoin (2006) 'The Spanish Empire and Its Legacy: Fiscal Re-distribution and Political Conflict in Colonial and Post-Colonial Spanish America' (Working Papers of the Global Economic History Network (GEHN) No.23/06: http://www.lse.ac.uk/collections/economichistory/GEHN/Default.htm).

Grenier, John (2005) *The First Way of War: American War Making on the Frontier* (Cambridge: Cambridge University Press).

Hamilton, Bernice (1963) *Political Thought in Sixteenth-Century Spain: A Study of the Political Ideas of Vitoria, De Soto, Suarez, and Molina* (Oxford: Clarendon).

Hamnett, Brian (1999) *A Concise History of Mexico* (Cambridge: Cambridge University Press).

Hanke, Lewis (ed.) (1964) *Do the Americas Have a Common History? A Critique of the Bolton Theory* (New York: Alfred A. Knopf).

Hanson, Simon G. (1938) *Utopia in Uruguay: Chapters in the Economic History of Uruguay* (New York: Oxford University Press).

Harris, Olivia (1995) '"The Coming of the White People": Reflections on the Mythologisation of History in Latin America,' *Bulletin of Latin American Research*, vol. 14, no. 1.

Hart, Albert Bushnell (1907) 'American Ideals of International Relations,' *American Journal of International Law*, vol. 1, no. 1 (January and April) pp. 624–35.

Hassig, Ross (1992) *War and Society in Ancient Mesoamerica* (Berkeley, CA: University of California Press).

Heaton, Herbert (1945) 'Yorkshire Cloth Traders in the US, 1770–1840' in G.D. Lumb and W.B. Crump (eds.) *The Thoresby Miscellany*, vol. 11 (Leeds: The Thoresby Society).

Heaton, Herbert (1946) 'Other Wests than Ours,' *Journal of Economic History*, vol. 6, no. 1 (supplement), pp. 50–62.

Hennessy, Alistair (1978) *The Frontier in Latin American History* (Albuquerque, NM: University of New Mexico Press).

Herr, Richard (1958) *The Eighteenth-Century Revolution in Spain* (Princeton, NJ: Princeton University Press).

Hilton, Stanley E. (1975) *Brazil and the Great Powers, 1930–1939: the Politics of Trade Rivalry* (Austin, TX: University of Texas Press).

Hilton, Stanley E. (1981) *Hitler's Secret War in South America, 1939–1945: German Military Espionage and Allied Counterespionage in Brazil* (Baton Rouge, LA: University of Louisiana Press)

Hobson, J.A. (1938) *Imperialism: A Study* [1902] (3rd ed. London: Unwin Hyman).

Holden, Robert H. (2004) *Armies Without Nations: Public Violence and State Formation in Central America, 1821–1960* (Oxford: Oxford University Press).

Holmes, Olive (1948) 'Argentina and the Dream of Southern Union,' in University of Texas Institute of Latin American Studies (ed.) *Political, Economic, and Social Problems of the Latin-American Nations of Southern South America* (New York: Greenwood Press).

Hsia, R. Po-Chia (1989) *Social Discipline in the Reformation: Central Europe, 1550–1750* (London and New York: Routledge).

Huntington, Samuel P. (1997) *The Clash of Civilizations and the Remaking of World Order* (New York: Simon & Schuster).

Huntington, Samuel P. (2004) *Who Are We? – America's Great Debate* (New York: Simon & Schuster).

Irigoin, Maria Alejandra, and Regina Grafe (2006) 'Bargaining for Absolutism: A Spanish Path to Nation State and Empire,' *University of Oxford Discussion Papers in Economic and Social History*, no. 65 (http://www.nuff.ox.ac.uk/Economics/History/).

James, C. L. R. (1938) *The Black Jacobins: Toussaint L'Ouverture and the San Domingo Revolution* (London: Secker and Warburg).

Johnson, James Turner (2006) 'The Just War Idea: the State of the Question,' *Social Philosophy and Policy*, vol. 23, no. 1, pp. 167–195.

Jones, Charles A. (1985) 'The Fiscal Motive for Monetary and Banking Legislation in Argentina, Australia and Canada before 1914,' in D.C.M. Platt and Guido di Tella (eds.) *Argentina, Australia and Canada: Studies in Comparative*

Development, 1870–1965 (Basingstoke: Macmillan in association with St. Antony's College, Oxford), pp. 123–38.

Jones, Charles A. (1987) *International Business in the Nineteenth Century: the Rise and Fall of a Cosmopolitan Bourgeoisie* (Brighton: Wheatsheaf).

Jones, Charles A. (1992a) 'British Capital in Argentine History: Structures, Rhetoric and Change,' in Alistair Hennessy and John King (eds.), *The Land that England Lost: Argentina and Britain, a Special Relationship* (London: I. B. Tauris)

Jones, Charles A. (1992b) *El reino unido y américa: inversiones e influencia económica* (Madrid: Editorial MAPFRE).

Jones, E.L. (1981) *The European Miracle: Environments, Economies, and Geopolitics in the History of Europe and Asia* (Cambridge: Cambridge University Press).

Jordan, Winthrop (1971) *White over Black: American Attitudes toward the Negro, 1550–1812* (Baltimore, MD: Penguin).

Jorgensen-Dahl, Arnfinn, et al. (1991) *The Antarctic Treaty System in World Politics* (London: Macmillan).

Kacowicz, Arie M. (1998) *Zones of Peace in the Third World: South America and West Africa in Comparative Perspective* (New York: State University of New York Press).

Kacowicz, Arie M. (2005) *The Impact of Norms in International Society: The Latin American Experience, 1881–2001* (Notre Dame, IN: University of Notre Dame Press).

Kamen, Henry (2002) *Spain's Road to Empire: The Making of a World Power, 1492–1763* (London: Allen Lane).

Kindleberger, Charles P. (1970) *Power and Money: the Economics of International Politics and the Politics of International Economics* (London: Macmillan).

Klein. Herbert S. (2003) *A Concise History of Bolivia* (Cambridge: Cambridge University Press).

Knorr, Klaus (1973) *Power and Wealth: the Political Economy of International Power* (New York: Basic Books).

Langley, Lester D. (2003) *The Americas in the Modern Age* (New Haven, CT & London: Yale University Press).

Leibniz, Gottfried Wilhelm (1972) 'Caesarinus Fürstenerius (De Suprematu Principum Germaniae)' [1677] in Patrick Riley (ed.), *Leibniz: Political Writings* (Cambridge: Cambridge University Press).

Lévy, Bernard-Henri (2006) *American Vertigo: On the Road from Newport to Guantanamo* (London: Gibson Square).

López, Vicente Fidel (2001) *La novia del hereje o La inquisición de Lima* [Buenos Aires, 1870] (Buenos Aires: Emecé Editores).

MacDonald, Callum A. (1986) 'The United States, Great Britain and Argentina in the Years Inmediately after the Second World War,' in Guido di Tella and D.C.M. Platt (eds.) *The Political Economy of Argentina, 1880–1946* (Basingstoke: Macmillan in association with St. Antony's College Oxford), pp. 183–200.

Mares, David R. (2001) *Violent Peace: Militarised Interstate Bargaining in Latin America* (New York: Columbia University Press).

Martí, José (2002) *Selected Writings* (Harmondsworth: Penguin).

Mignolo, Walter D. (2005) *The Idea of Latin America* (Oxford: Blackwell).

Morley, John (1905) *The Life of Richard Cobden* [1879] (London: Fisher Unwin).

Nettles, H. Edward (1928) 'The Drago Doctrine in International Law and Politics,' *Hispanic American Historical Review*, vol. 8 no. 2 (May), pp. 204–223.

Neufeld, E.P. (1969) *A Global Corporation: A History of the International Development of Massey-Ferguson Limited* (Toronto: University of Toronto).

North, Douglass C. (1966) *Growth and Welfare in the American Past: a New Economic History* (Englewood Cliffs, NJ: Prentice Hall).

North, Douglass C. (1973) *Rise of the Western World: a New Economic History* (Cambridge: Cambridge University Press).

North, Douglass C. (1981) *Structure and Change in Economic History* (New York: Norton).

O'Gorman, Edmundo (1961) *The Invention of America: An Inquiry into the Historical Nature of the New World and the Meaning of its History* (Bloomington, IN: Indiana University Press).

Olivos, Ruben (1996) *Tradition Matters: Modern Gaúcho Identity in Brazil* (New York: Columbia University Press).

Olney, Richard (1907) 'The Development of International Law: an address delivered before the American Society of International Law, April 20, 1907,' *American Journal of International Law*, vol. 1, no. 1 (January and April), pp. 418–430.

Olson, Mancur (1963) *The Economics of Wartime Shortage: a History of British Food Supplies in the Napoleonic War and World Wars I and II* (Durham, NC: Duke University Press).

Onuf, Nicholas G., and Thomas J. Johnson (1995) 'Peace in the Liberal World: Does Democracy Matter?' in Charles W. Kegley, Jr. (ed.) *Controversies in International Relations Theory: Realism and the Neoliberal Challenge* (New York: St. Martin's Press).

Pew Global Attitudes Project. Press release December 19, 2002. 'Among wealthy nations . . . US stands alone in its embrace of religion' (http://pew-global.org).

Pope Atkins, G. (1995) *Latin America in the International Political System* (3rd ed. Boulder, CO: Westview).

Putnam, Robert D. (2000) *Bowling Alone: the Collapse and Revival of American Community* (New York: Simon & Schuster).

Reinhard, Wolfgang (1989) 'Reformation, Counter-Reformation, and the Early Modern State: a Reassessment,' *The Catholic Historical Review*, vol. 75, no. 3 (July), pp. 383–404.

Robertson, A. H. and J. G. Merrills (1996) *Human Rights in the World: An Introduction to the Study of International Protection of Human Rights*, 4th ed. (Manchester: Manchester University Press).

Ronning, C. Neale (1963) *Law and Politics in Inter-American Diplomacy* (New York and London: John Wiley & Sons).

Rosworowski de Díez Canseco, Maria (1999) *History of the Inca Realm* (Cambridge: Cambridge University Press).

Rothwell, Donald (1966) *The Polar regions and the development of International Law* (Cambridge: Cambridge University Press).

Rubinstein, W.D. (1981) *Men of Property: the Very Wealthy in Britain since the Industrial Revolution* (London: Croom Helm).

Rubio, Mauricio (1998) 'Los costos de la violencia en América Latina: una crítica al enfoque económica en boga' (San Salvador), http://www.cerac.org.co/pdf/Comparative_Trends_in_Violent_Crime.pdf

Russett, Bruce (1993) *Grasping the Democratic Peace: Principles for a Post-Cold War World* (Princeton, NJ: Princeton University Press).

Sarlo, Beatriz (2000) 'The Modern City: Buenos Aires, the Peripheral Metropolis,' in Vivian Schelling (ed.) *Through the Kaleidoscope: the Experience of Modernity in Latin America* (London and New York: Verso).

Schelling, Vivian (ed.) (2000) *Through the Kaleidoscope: The Experience of Modernity in Latin America* (London and New York: Verso).

Schilling, Heinz (1995) 'Confessional Europe,' in Thomas A. Brady, Jr., Heiko A. Oberman and James D. Tracy (eds.) *Handbook of European History, 1400–1600: Late Middle Ages, Renaissance and Reformation*. Volume II-Visions, Programs and Outcomes. (New York and Köln: E. J. Brill).

Schumpeter, Joseph A. (1951) *Imperialism and Social Classes* [*c*. 1917] (Oxford: Blackwell).

Shelton, Dinah (1992) 'The Inter-American Human Rights System,' in Hurst Hannum (ed.) *Guide to International Human Rights Practice* (2nd ed. Philadelphia: University of Philadelphia Press).

Short, John Rennie (2001) *Representing the Republic: Mapping the United States, 1600–1900* (London: Reaktion Books).

Slatta, Richard W. (1997) *Comparing Cowboys and Frontiers* (Norman, OK and London: University of Oklahoma Press).

Souza Martins, José de (2001) 'Life in the Backlands and the Brazilian Popular Imagination' (Cambridge: unpublished paper presented at the Cambridge Conference on Brazilian Popular Art).

Spykman, Nicholas John (1942) *America's Strategy In World Politics: the United States and the Balance of Power* (New York: Harcourt Brace).

Stein, Gertrude (1966) *The Autobiography of Alice B. Toklas* [The Bodley Head, 1933] (Harmondsworth: Penguin).

Stern, Fritz Richard (1977) *Gold and Iron: Bismark, Bleichröder, and the Building of the German Empire* (London: Allen & Unwin).

Stiles, T. J. (2003) *Jesse James: Last Rebel of the Civil War* (London: Jonathan Cape).

Suzuki, Shogo (2005) 'Japan's Socialization into Janus-faced European International Society,' *European Journal of International Relations*, vol. 11, no. 1, pp. 137–164.

Sykes, Bryan (2006) *Blood of the Isles: Exploring the Genetic Roots of our Tribal History* (London: Bantam Press).

Telles, Edward E. (2004) *Race in Another America: the Significance of Skin Color in Brazil* (Princeton, NJ and Oxford: Princeton University Press).

Tocqueville, Alexis de (2000) *Democracy in America* (Chicago, IL and London: University of Chicago Press).

Trollope, Anthony (1968) *North America* [1862] (Harmondsworth: Penguin Books).

UNCTAD (1964) *Nueva política para el desarrollo. Informe de Raúl Prebisch [secretario general] a la Conferencia de la Naciones Unidas sobre Comercio y Desarrollo* (Mexico: Fondo de Cultura Económica).

United Nations University World Institute for Development Economics Research (http://www.wider.unn.edu/wiid/wiid.htm)

Vasquez, John A. and Marie T. Henehan (1992) *The Scientific Study of Peace and War: a Text Reader* (New York: Lexington).

Vernon, Raymond (1966) 'International Investment and International Trade in the Product Cycle,' *Quarterly Journal of Economics* vol. 80, no. 2 (May), pp. 190–207.

Vogel, David (1978) 'Why Businessmen Distrust Their State: The Political Consciousness of American Corporate Executives,' *British Journal of Political Science*, vol. 8, no. 1 (January), pp. 45–78.

Vonnegut, Kurt, Jr. (2000) *Slaughterhouse 5 or The Children's Crusade: A Duty-Dance with Death* [1969] (London: Vintage).

Whitehead, Laurence (2006) *Latin America: A New Interpretation* (New York and Houndmills: Palgrave Macmillan).

Wilkins, Philip S. (2003) 'Founding a Cambridge Cathedral: Yolande Lyne-Stephens, Canon Christopher Scott and the Church of Our Lady and the English Martyrs,' in Nicholas Rogers (ed.) *Catholics in Cambridge* (Leominster: Gracewing), pp. 106–118.

Williams, J. B. (1972) *British Commercial Policy and Trade Expansion, 1750–1850* (Oxford: Clarendon).

Williamson, Jeffrey G. (2003) 'Was It Stolper-Samuelson, Infant Industry or Something Else? World Tariffs, 1789–1938' (National Bureau of Economic Research, Cambridge MA: Working Paper 9656). http://www.nber.org/papers/w9656.

Wilson, R.G. (1971) *Gentleman Merchants: the Merchant Community in Leeds, 1700–1830* (Manchester and New York: Manchester University Press and Augustus M. Kelley).

Wohlforth, William H. (2007) 'Testing Balance-of-Power Theory in World History,' *European Journal of International Relations*, vol. 13, no. 2 (June), pp. 155–185.

World Bank (2004) *World Bank Atlas* (Washington DC: World Bank).

Zangrando, Robert L. (1991) 'About Lynching,' in Eric Foner and John A. Garraty (eds.) *The Reader's Companion to American History* (Boston, MA: Houghton Mifflin), pp. 684–686.

Zirker, Daniel (1994) 'Brazilian Foreign Policy and Sub-Imperialism during the Political Transition of the 1980s,' *Latin American Perspectives*, vol. 21, no. 1 (Winter), pp. 115–131.

INSTITUTE FOR THE STUDY OF THE
A M E R I C A S

UNIVERSITY OF LONDON · SCHOOL OF ADVANCED STUDY

The Institute for the Study of the Americas (ISA) promotes, coordinates and provides a focus for research and postgraduate teaching on the Americas – Canada, the USA, Latin America and the Caribbean – in the University of London.

The Institute was officially established in August 2004 as a result of a merger between the Institute of Latin American Studies and the Institute of United States Studies, both of which were formed in 1965.

The Institute publishes in the disciplines of history, politics, economics, sociology, anthropology, geography and environment, development, culture and literature, and on the countries and regions of Latin America, the United States, Canada and the Caribbean.

ISA runs an active programme of events – conferences, seminars, lectures and workshops – in order to facilitate national research on the Americas in the humanities and social sciences. It also offers a range of taught master's and research degrees, allowing wide-ranging multi-disciplinary, multi-country study or a focus on disciplines such as politics or globalisation and development for specific countries or regions.

Full details about the Institute's publications, events, postgraduate courses and other activities are available on the web at *www.americas.sas.ac.uk*.

Institute for the Study of the Americas
School of Advanced Study, University of London
31 Tavistock Square, London WC1H 9HA

Tel 020 7862 8870, Fax 020 7862 8886
Email *americas@sas.ac.uk*
Web *www.americas.sas.ac.uk*

INSTITUTE FOR THE STUDY OF THE
A M E R I C A S

UNIVERSITY OF LONDON · SCHOOL OF ADVANCED STUDY